THE FOUR FITS
OF HOLISTIC GROWTH

THE FOUR FITS
OF HOLISTIC GROWTH

Dr. Terrence D. Duncan

ISBN: 153093608X
ISBN 13: 9781530936083
Library of Congress Control Number: 2016906504
CreateSpace Independent Publishing Platform
North Charleston, South Carolina

TABLE OF CONTENTS

Introduction ·vii

Chapter 1   What are the Four Fits? · · · · · · · · · · · · · · · · · ·1
Chapter 2   The Spiritual/Mental Fit · · · · · · · · · · · · · · · · · ·**9**
        Axiom#1: I am very special, and I am unique
        regardless of my current situation. · · · · · · · · · · · · · 13
        Axiom #2: Do not be afraid to be the author of
        your destiny. · 15
        Axiom# 3: You do not have to go to school to
        become educated. · 21
        Axiom #4: The road to blocking your success is you · · · ·25
        Axiom #5: Turn your dreams into a
        vision, and make it a reality. · · · · · · · · · · · · · · · · 32
Chapter 3   The Emotional Fit ·40
        Axiom #6: Do not let last past failings prevent you
        from future opportunities · · · · · · · · · · · · · · · · · ·43
        Axiom #7: There is a difference between would
        like and want. · 48
        Axiom #8: Do not let your emotions get in the way
        in making a business decision. · · · · · · · · · · · · · · · 52
        Axiom #9: Take time to know yourself, and love yourself · ·58
        Axiom #10: Your love resume should be filled with
        as many accomplishments as your work resume · · · · · · 64
Chapter 4   The Financial Fit ·69
        Axiom #11: You cannot be a true millionaire unless
        you learn how to be a "thousandaire." · · · · · · · · · · · 72

               Axiom #12: Being debt-free does not send you to jail · · · · 76

               Axiom #13: You are your own brand. Learn how
               to invest in it. ·82

Chapter 5   The Physical Fit ·91

               Axiom 14: Find the right diet that is right for you · · · · ·93

               Axiom 15: Understand the stressors in your life · · · · · ·100

               Axiom 16: Your health depends on you, what will you
               do about it ·110

               Conclusion · 119

The Four Fits of Holistic Growth
Worksheets and Exercises · 125

Worksheet #1   Where Am I? ·127

Worksheet #2   I Am My Own Most Valuable Player (M.V.P.) · · · · · · ·129

Worksheet #3   The 12 Months of Progress · · · · · · · · · · · · · · · · ·131

Worksheet #4   The Road to Blocking Your Success is You,
               Flush out Negativity! ·134

Worksheet #5   Turning a Dream into a Vision and a
               Vision into Reality · 136

Worksheet #6   The Truth Should Not Hurt · · · · · · · · · · · · · · · · ·138

Worksheet #7   The Differences between Wants and Would
               Like is within Your Mind · · · · · · · · · · · · · · · · · ·139

Worksheet #8   Removing Your Emotions When Making
               Decisions Starts within You · · · · · · · · · · · · · · · ·140

Worksheet #9   Relax, Unwind, and Take Time for You · · · · · · · · ·142

Worksheet #10 Your Love Resume ·143

Worksheet #11 The Financial Cesspool – Credit Cards
               and Short Term Loans ·145

Worksheet #12 My Life's Vices ·147

Worksheet #13 Stress Management Comes from Stress Identification · · 149

Worksheet #14 My Life Matters ·151

Introduction

As we continue to move deeper and deeper into the 21st century, we have moved further away from who we are as a people. The challenges we face today are different from what we faced prior decades before. The challenges we face today are different from what we have encountered in the 1980s. The problems that are present in our lives are numerous regardless of race, religion, culture, and creed. An evaluation of sorts is necessary to meet these problems. By possessing the ability to assess who you are as a person, you will be able to face the challenges that exist in our daily lives.

I write this book based from my personal vantage point as an individual in his late 30's. I am educated, yet; I still feel the struggles that plague many of our communities. It is true whether you are a young mother of two trying to get through college, or a college student who is about to graduate from your local university. It is true whether you are happily married, but struggling in your job to find yourself; or if you are looking for a way to boost your struggling self-esteem or self-worth, I believe that this book is for you. By writing this book, I hope to contribute to the spiritual and emotional building that we all need. I also write this book from the vantage point of personal observations. These observations come from face to face encounters, third person point of views, and different interpersonal relationships developed over time.

I write this book with the burning passion and desire that has fueled me for years. Like many of my peers, and for those who are reading this book, I have yet to tap into the potential that makes me unique. I do not yearn to waste my years on this planet speculating and posturing about what I want my life to be. Instead, I aspire to reach my potential and attempt to do what I can do at a high level. My interactions with others have provided an excellent portrait. A framework for what issues plague our personal lives.

Similar to economics or saving for something significant such as a house or car or a special vacation, the challenges we encounter cannot resolve overnight. By taking sequential steps, by looking at our individual personalities in a microcosm-like fashion, we can cumulatively attempt to cure our societal and economic ails. This book attempts to contribute in ways that we commonly discuss amongst each other. I hope that for those who read this book can not only feel the passion provided behind the words but to analyze and genuinely assess how these viewpoints may assist in providing holistic health. Such growth in this fashion comes from your ability to merge the Four Fits into your daily lifestyle.

Throughout the book, I hope that you find these passages to be enlightening. I wrote this book as more of a conversation between you and me versus another self-help book that tells you everything you need to do to see the sunshine without first telling you how to open the window. The examples and the worksheets provided with each related axiom provides a compass for your ongoing personal development. During the process of writing this book, I shared some of these concepts with people who had varying backgrounds and different stories. I felt this was instrumental in ensuring this book is a conversation with you as a person. So, let us take this journey together, and I hope you find the Four Fits to be instrumental for your path towards personal development.

CHAPTER 1

What are the Four Fits?

THE FOUR FITS of Holistic Growth is a philosophy born on many segments of life. Ultimately, for whatever denomination or faith that you have, you can incorporate these core principles into your daily, weekly, and monthly lifestyle. In the end, we are responsible for our actions. Our actions then influence those around us, especially for those of us with children. By demonstrating a positive domino effect, we can slowly begin the evolutionary changes that we are so greatly destined to attain. At the same time, we slowly strip ourselves from the chains and shackles that have stunted our growth and potential that has plagued us.

I developed the Four Fits while pursuing my doctorate. I wanted to find a way to keep me grounded, and at the same time, find new ways to motivate me. I did not pursue my doctorate as a "look at me" status. I wanted to accomplish this because I believed in myself. I believed that I had what it takes to make it to the next level, yet at the same time, remove myself from the typical arrogance that people may perceive those who have accomplished this feat. Ultimately, I wanted to continue to remain grounded to who am I as a person and continue to relate to others who are seeking ways to improve themselves.

I feel that if someone reads this, they can relate and see that they can achieve whatever it is their heart desires. In this era of technology, the personable elements of that one-on-one diminish when we are looking for a new job, a new career, or just a change in our lifestyles. Instead, we have internet dating, online job recruiters, online job searches, submitting your resume online, etc. We now have so many social media outlets that it would take several lines to jot them down. You know the funny thing about it, is even though we have all these enhanced avenues to further ourselves for that career, second job, or just simply a job, we moved more and more away from what we can do to find what we need to enhance our personal resume. Not that resume for that one job downtown that pays close to six figures, but that resume for your life. Ask yourself this question, and be honest with yourself, if you stood before a panel of judges and interviewers, and they ask you to present your resume about your life, do you think that they would hire you? Now take the same panel of judges and interviewers, and you present your vocational and educational accomplishments before them, and I am confident that makes you feel that you have a legitimate chance for that job seen online on one of those job boards you kept checking online.

You see, I have a unique story to share about myself and this story is one reason why I was motivated to write the Four Fits. I was a career student. You know the one that graduated at 17 or 18 and went to school forever. I started working full time when I was 19 years old but tried to do too much. I flunked out of college not once, but twice. After sitting out for several years, I decided to give it another try. I remember feeling apprehensive and unsure. I asked myself was it worth it to go again. I knew that I had it in me, but was unsure that I had what it took to focus and lock in. Not only did I complete my bachelor's degree at 26, but I also obtained my MBA at 30.

During pursuing my MBA, I was laid off from the federal government. I had a child on the way, and I was scared because I never been out of work. I was forced to redefine myself. I will reiterate that I had no idea of what I wanted to do. At 30 years, I still was not 100% sure of what I wanted to achieve career-wise. At that point in time, I could have simply given up school again, and take whatever was available. However, I stayed the course and continued to find a job where it eventually became a good career move. I have several friends, as I am sure you do as well, who were not fortunate enough to rebound. For some who faced adversity of similar circumstances, their world collapsed. One mental mistake made after another. With the hard times, came a swarm of negativity and their lives spiraling out of control. It was difficult for me to see those close to me struggle. To this day, I still am concerned for those who have reached out to me because they struck a rough patch and was unsure as to how to get out.

The morale of this story is that it can be easy to give up. I had nowhere near the confidence or faith in myself back then as I do now. For me to continue to push through adversity, I found another gear. However, it took years to find that other gear. I had my share of struggles, some shared in this book, and it was not easy. I felt that the world was watching, and I had to perform. Therefore, for those who are currently in a rut or going through a string of bad luck, I challenge you to find that second gear. You, too, are on the stage and the world is watching.

It was easy to give up, reflecting back at it all. I did not know at that time that I had already laid the foundation of the Four Fits because I had to examine myself inside and out. It was easy to accept complacency. Accepting mediocracy was easy. It was easy to underachieve. Giving up was easy for me to do. While all that was easy, it was not easy to look at myself in the mirror every day and know that I can do so much more. It was not easy to know every day I had all this energy and spirit inside of me, waiting to exhale. It was not easy to know that I could do more but toiled. Therefore, I had to make a change. My journey that I am sharing with you; this set of ideas is more than a self-proclamation. I write this because I know that there are others like me out there trying to discover his or her journey in a way that you cannot simply Google. Sometimes, in the end, we need a good down to earth look at ourselves in the mirror and lift ourselves up in a manner where we can achieve what we wish to be, and for everything that we hope and strive to become.

The Four Fits is a model that does not appear in a matrix form. I created the Four Fits model to center on the holistic growth of an individual. In decades past, we did not have as many options for entertainment, references, communication, or have as many platforms as we do today to voice our concerns, fears, elation, and sorrow. In this world, we overload our brains with images, emotions, communication, information, and stimulation that it easy to lose yourself in the process. With this constant stimulation of our minds and spirits, sometimes to the point of overload, we continue to pull further and further away from our core values.

For those who were born in the 1970's and 80's, we can remember when TV was cut off with a rendition of "America the Beautiful" by Ray Charles and seeing a plane take off before the TV fades to the white noise static. We can even laugh reminiscing how getting HBO and more than say 10-12 channels was a big deal. Now we have many channels to choose from with a variety of specialty and theme-styled channels, along with many news stations that are on 24-hour cycles.

I am of the belief that while all these options are beneficial for our entertainment purposes, we continue to pull our spirit away from our minds. We have continued to lose our identity over the years. We are now in competition amongst our neighbors, friends, co-workers, associates, and even people we see on our social media updates that we do not even know personally. Why is this the case? It is simple, we are human, and are influenced and intrigued by something that we are currently either not experiencing or wanting to have is human nature.

The Four Fits is a simple model that you can incorporate into your life regardless of your race, religion, or financial stature. The design I created features a sphere that contains the Fits into different categories. When you try to figure out where do you fit in this sphere, try not to think of yourself in a box. Instead, think of yourself as a sphere, and within it, you are touching each segment and making it your personal "global" world. By thinking of yourself as a sphere, you can look at yourself holistically. In reviewing the sphere provided below, note how it is set up. Imagine you within this sphere and place yourself in the middle, thus connecting yourself infinitely without borders. From that point, you are creating yourself in a holistic plane.

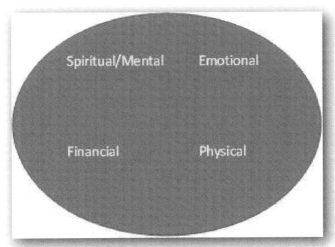

Four Fits of Holistic Growth

As stated before, you do not have to have three degrees, making six figures, or have a fancy house or car. You can do this in your 20s or 30s. You can do this after getting that job or career you had always wanted. You can do this even during retirement. The key to the Four Fits philosophy is much more than an ideology; it is a lifestyle.

When you read most self-help and motivational books, most books composed are at a time when the author is already successful. If you look at the bottom of their book, it may say New York Best-Selling author. By that time, he or she has amassed who knows in profits from their books and can look out their window knowing that they do not have to clock in for the day. I am writing this book at this moment, as an employee in the private sector. Even though I have a good job that pays well with perks, I felt that I could do more for myself, as well as help others.

I desire to write this book as an ongoing conversation between you and me. As such, I share these thoughts and words with you as I am practicing what I preach and seeing the wholesale changes that are occurring in my life now. I now can see a brighter future for myself in all four areas. I do hope that when you conclude reading this book, you will take each of the Four Fits and apply it your personal life, and I can assure that you will see the internal and external changes in your life.

When you think of the Four Fits, think of drawing a house on a piece of paper. When you do so, you will likely have a square-like design. Imagine taking some pegs and adding them to the corners of your drawn-out house. Those pegs represent the foundation of knowledge that you can build upon and then bridge additional pegs across your design. The Fits work in a manner where you can take most real-life situations and categorize them into a different Fit. For example, you can look at dealing with a complex work situation and apply an Emotional Fit for maintaining calm and poise while addressing the situation. Throughout the book, I will provide numerous anecdotes and examples of how the Fits can be beneficial in providing you a holistic growth of your inner being.

When utilizing the Four Fits, remember that you are not bound by certain sections of designated Fits. You can take an activity and find yourself crossing different planes. Being free from restriction from a particular trait or philosophy does nothing more but to restrict your growth as a person. If the average reader who read this book was 40 years old, could you imagine where you would be in life if you continued to have the same 21-year-old thinking? Although somewhat expected, a person goes through a certain maturation process of sorts, many of us still are blocked, constrained, constricted by no one other than ourselves! It is funny how we perceive so many obstacles to our desired growth to come externally when, in fact, the barriers are truly ourselves.

The question is how do we try to unblock our obstacles? How do we so "un-learn" what we have learned throughout our adult lives? This book may not have all the answers you seek; however, by embracing this thoughtful process, I have found myself being more at ease, more relaxed, and more in control of myself and my external circumstances than I was years ago, before I started to dwell on this fantastic concept. Throughout this book, you will encounter not only my personal examples of looking at different circumstances but from those who first started to hear about the Four Fits and how it had helped them develop holistic change internally and overall personal growth.

Change is not a concept that we embrace quickly. Change is a concept that may make us feel uncomfortable and uncertain. It is easier to go with what we know rather than try something different. It is simpler to fall back to what we are aware after trying something new after losing the momentum to maintain the change. Notice how I did not use the term quit. I chose to avoid negative words and concepts during my personal growth and use of the Four Fits. Embracing negative words and thoughts will lead to ideas that are more negative. This cycle of negativity will eventually cascade to a mountain of frustration, disdain, and ultimately throwing in the towel. By saying that you quit, you are saying that you give up. If you are reading this book, I am certain that none of us is in the business of trying to give up.

Whether you occasionally or often get off track, it is ok if you find a way to regain your momentum. Imagine that you are cooking something for the first time something that you may have saw on a cooking show on your local news channel, or on cable. The first time you try cooking this item, especially without a recipe like this author here, it may not look visually appealing nor taste as good as they make it seem on television. What do you do? You find yourself saying, "Well, I tried cooking this and it did not come right so I will not try it again." This statement is not necessarily true. What happens is that you have that inner determination that kicks in to try it again some time later. The more you try, the better the meal. Soon, everyone will be raving about this new dish to the point that you are bringing it to family and social gatherings. I am sure that you are not bringing that dish you made the first time to the same gatherings. In other words, keep trying. Keep practicing that recipe that is your inner self until you are pleased enough to the point you are willing to show the world who you are as a person inside and out.

How does it feel when you receive a sincere compliment? Normally, it is unexpected, you feel good, and you naturally smile. The process of hearing a compliment with your ears, treating it with your brain, your smile, and the neurological effect or "glow" that you feel throughout your body is very pleasing and rewarding. If you continue to work on your inner self, you will learn how to compliment yourself naturally by recognizing how much of a better person that you are and how that projects toward others.

Ultimately, the Four Fits is a guide that helps you reach that natural compliment. Change does not happen overnight, but if you go back and read certain sections again, and work on those areas, you will find holistic growth and awareness. As a result, your interactions with others, whether it is a relationship, business transaction, or social settings will have a smooth, steady flow to it, and you will find yourself more naturally at peace.

I use the Four Fits as a guide for my personal development. In achieving these Fits, I have discovered the tangible and intangible effects of accomplishing holistic change. Where I used to be quick-tempered, reactive, and often upset at certain circumstances, I have become more reserved, at peace, and better equipped mentally to address most if not all situations. While it took a while to get accustomed to this line of thinking, this now comes to me as a natural instinct. When I evaluate myself after a possible situation had occurred, I feel like I have scored myself consistently well. I find myself enjoying life a little more, as well as strengthening my relationships with friends and loved ones.

The holistic developments I have discovered within myself have emitted a different energy that people feel more comfortable in their interactions with me no matter the circumstances. Despite this level of personal development achieved, I continue to work and work on this, because I, like you, am not a finished product. I do so hope that you find this book and this mindset to be helpful for you regardless of age, race, religion, and educational/financial status.

Before you dive into this book, I want you to take a break and ask yourself these questions. Where do you find yourself spiritually/mentally, emotionally, physically, and financially? What areas do you find yourself feeling that you need to improve on the most? For your benefit, as I do understand everyone has different methods of learning, I have created handouts in the worksheets that you may use to help keep track about your personal development. In Worksheet #1, you will find a brief exercise where you can jot your answers down to this question with additional information where you may write notes.

CHAPTER 2

THE SPIRITUAL/MENTAL FIT

THE SPIRITUAL AND mental elements of this Fit are interrelated in that I did not see the point of separating them as different talking points. However, both concepts in this Fit help lay the first segment of the foundation of your new home, which internally and externally is you! When you can achieve all fits in sync, you will have gained a larger sense of being. The question begs itself, how can you achieve being whole when the most precious cargo in your personal life needs healing?

There is a connection between spirituality and mentality. When I speak of spirituality as one of the Four Fits, I talk about it as your core being. Spirituality is your connection to yourself and awareness within. Spirituality and being religious are two different concepts. As the intended audience for this book is to reach everyone regardless of culture, race, creed, or religion, I will refrain from enforcing religious beliefs and principles. The only exception to this statement is that you should continue to believe in your religious principles. I, myself, am a Christian; however, I have respect for the feelings and beliefs that others may have. The journey to achieve a holistic being from within relies on these four principles. Once you find yourself holistically, I firmly believe that your religious beliefs and understanding of your religion enhances.

By being religious, you succumb yourself to a larger faith and cause. Although there is nothing wrong in believing a higher power, your sense of spirituality may enhance your religious beliefs and values. When you focus solely on your religious beliefs, you follow the core tenants, beliefs, and values found in that religion. However, if you lack a connection within yourself spiritually, you will have difficulties understanding your place and role in your religion. You may also likely experience conflicts with yourself with your religious beliefs, while you struggle with making yourself more balanced spiritually.

Spirituality assists your mental health. Some people find that their spirituality provides hope and support during difficult times[1]. Finding your spirituality can come in a variety of ways from living with a set of codes and morals. By having a set of laws and morals, you develop your personal spiritual compass. Interpersonal relationships nurture your spirituality. Negative associations or negative energy may affect your core being, despite how strong you may feel you are as a person.

Spirituality and mental health are interrelated as your connection to your core being could influence your overall mental health negativity or positively. If your mental health is poor, you may tend to become more frustrated, angrier, despondent, a high degree of uncertainty about yourself, and an imbalance of social interests. Think of this as you are at the edge of a swimming pool in a hotel and you want to jump in, but you know the water is frigid. The result is that you slowly put your body in, mainly your feet, and then pull it out because you perceive you are cold. After this internal cat and mouse, you eventually get in the water. Yes, everyone is entitled to up and down days, as this is a part of life. If you do not have a positive mental health outlook on life and yourself, the struggles become more intense and profound.

The mental element is the second half of this first Fit. As stated before, your mental well-being helps provide clarity and focus, or lack thereof, when attempting to achieve your goals and your everyday routine in life. Mental health does not necessarily mean that you have depression or bipolar disorder, which are commonly associated when people engage in conversations about mental health. In actuality, there

---

1 Spirituality and Mental Illness http://mhcd.org/sites/default/files/asset_files/ Spirituality%20and%20Mental%20Illness%20%20Fact%20Sheet%20-%20%20 Rethinking%20Mental%20Illness.pdf

appears to be an insufficient discussion of mental health in modern day discussions. As well, when speaking to numerous people, it seems that most are not able to ascertain a particular reason or rationale for how they are feeling. Instead, people are lost in a wave of emotion, and not able to produce more foresight or thought into their actions.

Developing a healthy mental profile is as important as taking care of your physical health. Thus, the reason why the Spiritual/Mental Fit appears in this book first as it sets the table for addressing other fits. Let us say you are attempting to lose weight to improve your physical appearance and overall health. Lack of mental engagement into the commitment it takes to lose the weight (i.e. exercise, dieting, lifestyle decisions, etc.) means that you will likely have difficulty losing weight.

Similar to taking a test for school or even for a job, if your confidence is relatively shaky or you exhibit poor test taking skills, you have a mental block that is preventing you from taking these tests. Trust me; I can relate to that. When I took statistics, I took the course a couple of times because I had this mental block and a fear of statistics. Even taking doctorate level statistics, I would seek out others to help me understand what I was more than capable of doing. After spending thousands of dollars for tutors and assistance, I ultimately became frustrated and empowered to learn it on my own. Amazingly enough, not only was I able to do it, I was able to understand it, and on some level, can "speak" in the language of statistical probabilities. Therefore, I had to change my mental health to become more confident and driven, to take my education to the next level.

Another example to highlight how spiritual and mental are interrelated, look to those who had survived cancer, a heart attack, and other debilitating illnesses. If you read the stories of these survivors, which you can read on the internet or merely ask a survivor in person, what you will hear are common themes. The will to live and the reason why they wanted to live. The reasons may vary from person to person; however, the constant is a combination of the spiritual and mental strength that helped them through the toughest stretches. The spiritual and mental resiliency provided them strength through chemo, rehab, or the combination of prescription medication needed daily. Under the Spiritual/ Mental Fit, if one or both were not balanced or healthy enough, it is likely that they would not survive. Although I am not stating that you are in a life or death situation, life does provide the greatest anecdotes. Seek, listen, and learn from those around you, and you will be amazed that deep down, you are not much different from them. You are also not that much different from me, as well. I openly confess that I am not much different from you.

For those that I have provided life coaching sessions, I have encouraged those who seek to accomplish their dreams to change their mindset as my first recommendation. Many of the people that I have coached do not realize their true potential and ability. Everyone has their personal stories of suffering, challenges, and setbacks. The beauty of life is to not embrace those setbacks but to use them to help guide you on your path. Believing in yourself in times when times are down. Failure to understand who you are as a person deep down will create more challenges than opportunities. Developing a positive mental being, along with a connected spiritual sense, is critical in your overall personal development.

I use the word personal development similar to how employers use the word human resources. I ask that you do not look at yourself as a business entity that steadily creates inputs and outputs. The reality of life is that the majority of us will have to work to survive. We live in a society where our basic needs and our desired wants are obtained through earning money. Some are driven more by money than others are, and because of that, people pour more energy into building their work resume than their personal resume. If we consumed as much energy into ourselves as what we pour into our job, career, or whatever you are trying to accomplish externally into ourselves, it would be a beautiful sight to see. Thus, the word personal development is more appropriate in understanding who we are as a person and how we seek to "promote" ourselves.

Personal development should be an ongoing process; regardless of where you are today, and where you were five years ago. Your goal is to provide yourself more opportunities in life by having a healthy spiritual outlook and a solid mental health profile that allows you to keep going no matter what you are going through. Assessing your ongoing personal development is achieved in a variety of ways. In this book, I provide you tools of your personal growth. Once you can master the tools of your own development process, accepting your place in life and the flow of things become more fluid and clearer.

I am an astute observer of people. I love to listen to their stories and hear what makes them unique. Ultimately, how much money you have, how much education you had attained, or the type of home that you are currently living in does not matter, we are all very special and unique. One thing to keep in mind is that everyone had to start somewhere. The Four Fits will help you get to that point you are trying to reach. So, with that said, let us say to our inner being the following axiom.

AXIOM #1: I AM VERY SPECIAL, AND I AM UNIQUE REGARDLESS OF MY CURRENT SITUATION.

When listening to these stories, I have been able to detect pain. I have been able to see the scars by the complexities of life. Life is hard. There are a small percentage of us in this country, better yet, the world that was born with a lack of worries. For those who profess that they have no worries, that statement is so far from the truth. We are humans; we are always obsessing, fretting, and concerned about something one way or another. The key is how we let this either be the iron that sharpens your resolve or be the waves that cascade over the rocks in the ocean carrying your personal boat to a place of chaos and uncertainty.

Remember, as stated before, I have been on both spectrums. I have seen my personal boat crash many times, only to salvage myself repeatedly by not wanting to give up, not wanting to lose. In developing this Fit to work within your inner self, try using this thought process: Write down what you have accomplished so far in life. I have included this exercise under Worksheet #2. Take as much time as you want to jot down 12 things that you feel were significant accomplishments in your life. As we continue to develop this Fit together, it will take some time. Do not fret, if you cannot accomplish it all in your first setting or even after your first reading in this section. The key is to acknowledge not only who you are, but also what you accomplished.

To determine the 12 significant events, you should first understand that your life has meaning. I do not expect anyone to have one reading of the book and say I have mastered this entirely new mindset. This mindset is similar to taking a cooking course at a local community college learning how to make something you enjoy. Remember the reference about that recipe that you have been trying to nail down. Normally, you are not going to nail it the first time. Instead, it takes time. Therefore, your list of 12 should take time. Do not be surprised that you have to go back and rewrite the list repeatedly after you gave this more thought. That is a great thing if you have to keep going back to the list to change what you had before because you are in the initial process of acknowledging your self-worth. This process is as similar as making that initial deposit into a financial investment account of your choice, patiently waiting for the investment to pay off.

We currently live in a society fueled by social media, instant gratification, and other responsibilities and obligations where time sped up on us. We find ourselves always rushing to take care of this and that. While all of this is happening, we often tend to ignore ourselves in the process. Because time sped up on us, we find ourselves staring at the mirror and not liking what we see. Trust me, I have been there and done that myself. The beauty of life is that as long as you have breath in your lungs, you are more than capable to continue to write your destiny.

Take a moment to reflect on your 12 accomplishments in your life. It is amazing, regardless of the age you are currently, what stands out as achievements in your life. Often, in this era, we are so rushed and hurried that we fail to take a moment to take a step back and notice what we accomplished. Instead, we continue to barrel ahead to what we feel what we want or need best. Whether you believe it or not, there is a distinct difference between wanting and needing. I discuss these differences in more detail later in the book.

The goal of Worksheet #2 is two-fold. To map out what should be our next significant achievement, we should be able to recall not only what we accomplished, but remember the painful steps of getting there. For example, let us say that you have completed your bachelor's degree. The paths of obtaining a bachelor's degree are numerous for each person, and no two roads are the same, but the personal struggles mirror that person's degree of difficulty. The difficulties of obtaining a bachelor's degree straight out of high school in a sense are no more different than earning a bachelor's degree as a single parent of two at the age of 27. The paths were different, but that person's individual story to reaching this accomplishment was as stressful as another person's journey. One way of working on your Mental Fit is to realize that you are the author of your personal story. You may not necessarily have to write it down as a book or discuss it in different media, but you are responsible for your screenplay of your life. To that end, I share another axiom.

Axiom #2: Do not be afraid to be the author of your destiny.

At the bottom of Worksheet #2, you will find Exercise #3. Take a moment to glance at it, but do not complete it now. Now is a good moment to take another moment to reflect on where you are, where you have been, and where you would like to go in life. Under the Mental Fit, you should realize that often our biggest enemy is ourselves. Our mind is a powerful instrument that we nurture and cultivate it to help shape our views, opinions, biases, perceptions, etc. One of the primary purposes of the Four Fits is to help you understand that you can develop your mind in ways that help you remain connected to all things around you spiritually/mentally, emotionally, physically, and financially. Doing so can help you achieve the holistic change you have been seeking to accomplish for so long, but was unsure of how to reach it.

Before completing the exercise, let us clear our minds for a moment and provide a couple of scenarios in your mind to think to consider. We will start with something that is relatively easy and applies to essentially everyone who is reading this book, cooking. You are having guests over for dinner, and you want to have a nice, simple dinner planned. What do you do? Your first inclination is to say you are going to the store. Well, what are you going to cook? What are you going to buy? Will just running to the store at 4:00 p.m. give you enough time to prepare for dinner at 6:00 p.m.?

More than likely, the answers will vary from reader to reader. The more experienced "cooks" will not fret over something like this. However, those who may not be the most experienced of cooks will have some stress trying to figure out what to cook, as well as how to have everything prepared in a short amount of time. What is the simple way to prepare for this event? Simple, it is planning. When you achieved your 12 significant accomplishments, it did not happen overnight. Let me repeat it, and then I want you to repeat it to yourself, "IT DID NOT HAPPEN OVERNIGHT!" Now that we have gotten that out of the way, we can focus on this exercise. To work on your Spiritual Fit, you will need to understand that nothing in life is easy. If everything were easy, you probably would not be reading this book, and I probably would not be writing this book as well. Seriously, look at your accomplishments and ask yourself, what did you accomplish that came to you with ease?

Take the time and think about what you would like to achieve in the next 12-15 months. The purpose of this exercise is for you to identify what you would like to achieve in the next 12-15 months and chart how you would like to achieve it. Being thoughtful on how you would like to accomplish your next set of goals will provide a road map to your success. For example, you may want to go on a vacation to an all-expense-paid trip to a resort of your choosing. If you do not have the money readily available, how do you prepare to take this vacation a year from now?

The more reasonable way to pay for this trip is preparation. Use of a budget and savings plan (a Financial Fit) may help you achieve your goal. Even though it sounds easy on paper, saving money is not as easy as it seems despite an individual's earning potential. As of 2015, 29% of Americans do not have any emergency savings regardless of the size of their paychecks[2]. Therefore, their means of paying for this kind of vacation getaway would be dependent on increasing their debt or using other ways to pay off their vacation that would put more financial stress on them in the short and intermediate term.

Another scenario to put in perspective before completing Exercise 3 is someone's desire to lose weight. Maybe that person wants to lose weight for a wedding, or for his or her individual self-esteem. Let us say that this person wants to lose 15 pounds in 6 months. While we can look at the numbers and say the obvious trap words "Oh, you can do that," that person may realize that it may not be as easy as she or he may think by the beginning of the second month. I am sure that everyone who is reading this book is thinking this person is not exercising right, eating right, or have other issues that could affect their goal of losing weight. Even though that we know that every person is different, one truth is that speaking on something and not taking action to accomplish it will not work. Speaking the words into existence, as easy as it is believable, is hard to attain unless there is action. Therefore, if you are not putting in the effort, hard work, or sacrifices, how can you reach this significant accomplishment?

Refer to Exercise 3. I would like for you to not only have you complete these exercises in this book but understand the thought process that best fits for you. To achieve a significant milestone or milestones, you must be able to map out realistic and attainable goals. You cannot

---

2 "Americans Still Lack Savings Despite Bigger Paychecks." Jannon Herron. http://www.bankrate.com/finance/consumer-index/americans-still-lack-savings-despite-wage-growth.aspx

accomplish a four-year degree program in the third month of your first year. It is not realistic. Receiving your degree is; however, it will take time. Therefore, most of what we would like to accomplish in life will take time.

One thing to keep in mind during this process of this Spiritual Fit is that you will undoubtedly face adversity and hard times. You will face something that will throw you for a loop or something that will pop up and distract you from your objectives and goals. I hate to tell you; that is life. I have spoken with many successful people and listened to their stories. One common theme I have heard repeatedly is that it was not easy. Hardships happened whether it was personal, family, or financial. I have yet to meet someone that said that he or she woke up one morning and had the world at his or her feet. Everyone must keep pushing somehow, someway to achieve his or her goals and objectives, and eventually reach that main prize. So, my message to you is that even though life will throw you some curveballs, as long as you have breath in your lungs, fight and keep fighting to achieve what you are striving to attain.

You may come up with several goals to accomplish in a 12-, 15-month stretch. As stated before, you will face obstacles in life. The purpose of this exercise is to allow you some leeway to accomplish your goals so that you do not feel deterred from your vision. If you are trying to save money for that trip you wanted, and you have little savings, a curve ball may happen. Knowing Murphy's Law, a curve ball WILL happen. The feeling of having an obstacle pop up while you are trying to save for your trip will provide you some sense of anxiety, despair, and maybe a desire to give up. I am here to tell you that there is nothing wrong feeling this way and that it happens to more people than you think to do. I, too, have moments of anxiety and inadequacies that surface from time to time. However, in my heart, I know that I cannot give up and will keep pushing on, and I encourage you to do the same.

Similar to thinking of your 12 significant accomplishments, take your time in coming up with 12 actionable goals that you wish to achieve within a year. The purpose of this exercise; however, is that you must find 12 things throughout a calendar year for things that you can reasonably control. A Mental Fit to keep in mind is that your mind can be your blessing and your curse. You have to train your mind to think of and to seek great things. If you set your mind to achieve something that you cannot control, you will more than likely drive yourself crazy trying to accomplish those goals. For example, if you are currently unemployed or under-employed, putting down by the 7th month that you plan to have a prestigious job by that time is likely not going to happen. If your significant 12 has not trended you towards that path, you will be frustrated trying to figure out why you continue to be stuck. You must be able to have something more attainable, more realistic that you can have small victories to keep you enthusiastic about your personal development. To land that prestigious job, which is possible, will take long-term planning. Therefore, you must take the smaller victories to get there. As a result, you may have in your first three months of your new 12, highlight how you are going to research jobs that fit your profile; research colleges or programs that can assist you towards achieving this long-term goal; or find a place to volunteer to get more experience that may pay off in the long run. Jotting down these items makes your plan clearer and concise, and begin to give you realistic hope that you may achieve your long-term goals.

Never be afraid to take control of your destiny. In life, we will encounter numerous obstacles and challenges. Sometimes, we face flashpoints at a critical juncture in our lives. Flashpoints occur when a moment or opportunity forces you to make a choice. When you make that particular choice, your path follows that next line towards the road to your destiny. Flashpoints exist as a moment in time when that particular decision leaves a lasting imprint in your mind. In embracing the spiritual fit, the more you encounter a particular flashpoint in time, you will become more aware of that critical juncture, and make a decision that guides you into the destiny that you so desire.

Ultimately, your list of 12 goals to accomplish in the next 12-15 months should be attainable for you. Small baby steps and minor victories can do a lot for your psyche. Try setting a day each month to look at your current progress towards achieving each of your 12 goals. If you are a natural procrastinator or tend to get discouraged if you do not accomplish certain things, try setting your review date to the middle of the month versus the end of the month. By setting your review date in the middle of the month, you allow yourself ample time to rally yourself to achieving your monthly goal.

Do not try to overreach when listing your 12 goals. One of the biggest issues in attempting to accomplish our goals is that we are aware of our limitations and set ourselves up for disappointment. Our ability to become more self-aware and spiritually connected within is blocked unrealistic expectations at this moment. For example, you cannot walk into a luxury car dealership with average credit and a small down payment and expect to walk out with a favorable car note. You may look at this example and say what did you expect? Unfortunately, many of us have this type of logic, but not such an extreme. Therefore, the mindset you should take in completing this exercise is simplicity, but something meaningful. We want to create an ongoing sense of accomplishment, not a constant sense of frustration.

Another key in setting the review day for your monthly goals is to allow you to enjoy yourself. Doing so addresses a critical piece of your Spiritual/Mental Fit. Being able to refresh and recharge is as important as your determination to accomplish your goals. If you continue to press, you will burn out. Stepping back and taking time for you is important for your general well-being. Taking a break and taking time for yourself helps you re-connect with your spirit and soul. Taking a break may also reinvigorate you into whatever your desired goal may be. You will see that taking a break and taking time for you discussed throughout this book.

Axiom# 3: You do not have to go to school to become educated.

Coming from someone with a doctorate, yes, I will say this and will say this with conviction, you do not have to go to school to become educated. Although I do encourage and believe that people should go to college, you must understand the reason why you are going to college. I find this axiom to be the most interesting because many people will invest in college through many means, but learning is an ongoing process that ranges from free to little investment on your behalf. We all understand the value of higher education, but mentally we do not grasp how we often fall into a trap regarding seeking this valued prize.

Personally, I ran up a significant amount of student loans debt to get where I am today. Although I am fortunate to have the means to pay down my financial obligations, I look back at some decision made where I could have saved myself some painful moments. Recall the previous discussion regarding the term flashpoints. I encountered some trying to get my first degree. Earlier, I mentioned that I flunked out of college twice. It was not due to lack of intelligence, which was always there. It was due to lack of discipline and not knowing when to separate what was a priority and what was a perceived want.

Without going into explicit details, I had many things pulling at me at one time. Working full time, raising a family, and going to school full time at night was not one of my greater ideas at the time. Now, this was before the popularity and convenience of distance learning. During my sabbaticals, I continued to maintain my employment. To this day, some of my best learning experiences were not in the classroom; it was during my regular, everyday encounters with my co-workers, supervisors, peers, etc. From that point, I was able to learn more about myself and make myself more spiritually aware. Although I did not know this at the time, I was utilizing the Spiritual/Mental Fit throughout those crucial years before returning to school and making it to the finish line.

Life sets the table for an ongoing learning experience. We tend to become so absorbed in ourselves that we tend not to pay attention to the little clues scattered throughout our daily lives. Try to seek information that you do not know so you can make yourself more aware inside and out. In this era of information technology, social media, and the Internet, there are so many ways to learn more. Expanding your knowledge is an essential element of your mental fit. In college, for most intents and purposes, you receive a set curriculum to hone your particular skill set. For those who have gone through college, we can all agree that some of these courses had nothing to do with our overall degree. Seek information on your own to fill in those gaps.

By filling in the gaps, you are unknowingly providing yourself additional opportunities in life. If you are struggling with finances, you do not have to go to college to learn about financial management. If you happen to read about stocks and mutual funds, you do not have to be an accounting or finance major. If you want to be a chef, signing up for a culinary school is not mandatory. Although for certain jobs, there are certain requirements, you must understand, you are your private employer. You are in charge of your human resources, accounting, counseling, benefits, etc. Working on the Spiritual/Mental fit is not a college course or prerequisite. It is something that you can do on your own free or with little to no investment.

Self-awareness comes from exposure to events or learned experiences that expand your consciousness. When you were a child, you thought that your immediate neighborhood and community was similar to other places throughout the country. When you saw the news or sports on TV, you would notice how it is brighter in one part of the country while you looked at the window and noticed that it was dark. The older you became, and the more knowledge that you possessed about the world expanded your self-awareness. Now, you see something live on TV from the Central time zone at 8 p.m. and recognize that whatever shown on the television has a moderate amount of daylight assists you to determine that they are more than likely on the West Coast.

Developing an understanding of your surroundings, environment, and yourself creates an enhanced sense of self-awareness. An enhanced self-awareness creates additional opportunities that you may not know even existed. Rather than accept your life as a victim of circumstances or a product of your environment, try to break those norms, and invest in yourself to become more self-aware. I challenge you to become more aware of not only what is going on in your world but why. Listen to your body, trust your eyes, and interpret what you are hearing. In developing the spiritual fit, self-awareness is an important tool in the journey towards your personal development.

There are benefits when learning on your own. Your research and learning are tools for your personal development. When we continue to live in a box, we do not see what is outside the box. One of the key concepts of not only this Fit, but all of the Four Fits, is to conceptually find ways to think outside the box and expand our internal and external awareness. There is a wealth of information available. Within your list of 12 goals for the next year, I challenge you to research articles, blogs, journals, or short documentary or video to expand your awareness of what you are trying to accomplish.

The mind and the spirit are amazing when you take a step back and think about it. You learned how to swim, drive, ride a bike, or a ride a motorcycle. Remember the apprehension you had when you originally started to how you feel now whenever you do any of the above activities. You trained your mind and body to accomplish these feats. Your fears that you had in the past soon turned to relaxation, exhilaration, or a relief of stress. Those feelings come from within your spirit.

Your path towards an ongoing sense of self-awareness is not necessarily in a classroom. Even those who graduated and strived to become successful or holistic often seek this route by continuous learning. This type of learning can come from networking, reading books, engaging people who may have different social circumstances to continue to add to what they already knew. You should never try to be stagnant in life. To achieve your accomplishments and continued self-development, stagnation is not an option.

If you feel like you are in a state of complacency, do not be afraid to ask yourself and attempt to identify the reason why you feel stuck. Although the purpose of the Four Fits is not to make you successful financially, you should always try to define your life as a successful internally. Avoid the groupthink, and learn to live, learn, laugh, and love outside the box. Remember, the Four Fits concept is a guide to make your life whole and live without boundaries. Accepting that you are stuck will continue to confine you in that box that you may subconsciously not know that you are living.

Some of the material that you will encounter in your path of self-awareness may present to you some cold hard truths. Some may hurt. As long as you continue to have life in your lungs, you are more than capable to beat the odds and statistics that define others. Keep in mind that success and change do not happen overnight. The changes that you seek in your life will take time. I would like to repeat this saying again, "The changes that you seek in your life will take time." Your path towards self-awareness and unlocking the beauty that lies within your spirit take practice, managing your ups and downs, and overcoming your obstacles. You should feel neither deterred nor defeated when you meet the challenges that confront you as long as you have the will to succeed.

Now take that same concept and apply it to your 12 goals. You have to practice and train your mind and spirit to embrace the challenge that lies ahead. If you are trying to save money for a three-day road trip to somewhere different, do not try to say, I want to make a drive to Chicago. Conduct some research on the city, check out websites that feature tourist attraction, and take advantage of some special rates or other specials that you may see in your discount apps. The action you take not only helps contribute to your Financial Fit, but it will also provide you some additional information to consider when planning your trip, rather than just going and making it up on the fly.

As a guide to assist you in your 12-month journey, please refer to Worksheet 3. In this worksheet, highlight the goal that you wish to accomplish for each month. Under that goal, I challenge you to research two to three things that you think may be beneficial for your personal development. As you progress through each month, you will continue to populate this worksheet. This worksheet will not only remind you the steps that you took to assist your overall holistic growth, but it will also help you become focused and organized on the overall path towards embracing your mental and spiritual strength in achieving your goals. As each month progresses and for each accomplishment you reached, I am confident that you will dig deeper and deeper into learning new things and stimulating your mind to think more and more outside the box.

Axiom #4: The road to blocking your success is you

Imagine that you are about to take a road trip. You take off, and after a couple of hours, you run into a sign that says the interstate is closed, and follow the detour. You are not accustomed to driving often, so you have a sense of trepidation and panic starting to creep in. You look off to your right, and you can see that by taking the next exit, you can hop on the overpass and then turn around to head home. Another option is that you chance it by taking the rural, two-lane roads for approximately 45 minutes with a high chance that you will have no cell phone coverage.

Life is similar to taking a long road trip where sometimes not everything works the way you would prefer. You will encounter obstacles, roadblocks, and other oddities that will frustrate you. Despite this, the only force that is truly stopping you is you. Go back to your list of 12 accomplishments that you completed the second exercise. Take one of the twelve and think about what you went through to reach that significant achievement or milestone.

In an era where society and people clamor for everything to happen right away, more often than not, the chances of that occurring are slim. Similar to trying to bake a cake, or the distance it takes to travel from your home to your relative's house far away, a series of events or sequences must occur for you to reach your final destination. The moment your mind conceives what it is that you wish to accomplish; the process must take place to achieve that objective. For example, in writing this book, I have provided a conception of what I would like this book to resemble; however, speaking on it will not help complete the book. I must have a plan, and the patience to finish this book for you to read it. As you are reading this book, take note that it took days, weeks, months, and a lot of starting and stopping to complete it. At the end of this book, I will feel a sense of accomplishment, and mark this off as one of my projected goals for my next 12 months.

Your road of life will continue to have potholes, traffic jams, and construction. There will be moments where you will feel like you stuck in perpetual motion. Moments will occur when you feel like you made a wrong turn and your personal GPS appears to be off. That is where you must search within spirit to find that compass, your GPS to get back on the road and heading towards your destination. Remember, if everything in life were easy, we would all be swimming in wealth, perfect health, promotions and raises happening like clockwork. Life does not work that way.

You and only you can define where your road of life will take you. You shape your destiny and own future. For every roadblock you encounter, you must summon the strength and inner resolve to overcome the adversity that you face in life. We will discuss the Financial Fit later; however, finances often contribute as one of the major roadblocks in a person's life. I admit it was one of my main obstacles as well. However, you must realize first that you have set your destiny into a life of debt and financial hardships. A variety of reasons exists as to why this may happen, and each person will have their life story. However, you must remember that for the most part, no one placed a gun to our head and told us to incur significant amounts of debt. Often we attempt to solve our problems in a reactionary state of mind. Often, we try to do so in a quick and ineffective fashion, only to make that road in our life littered with larger potholes.

Negative energy affects you in a variety of ways. Even if you are an optimistic person in general, negativity affects you consciously and subconsciously. For example, you are thinking about buying a car. You have an interest in one particular car model, but you heard on the news and through other people that this particular model had a recall. The recall involved a defective part that created numerous accidents. Even though the probability of being involved in one of these accidents with this particular model is slim to none, you embrace the negativity associated with this model and forgo buying it, even though this model has had a history of a superb safety record before the recall.

The flood of negative images affects your decision-making at times. Think of that time when you were going to check out a particular restaurant or movie and your close friend tells you how horrible it was. When you have the option to attend that same movie or restaurant, the same negative imagery is in your mind. However, when you decided to check it out yourself, you realize that it was quite a different experience than what you had expected. Why did you expect this to be a bad idea? It is simple, the seeds of negativity implanted in your mind already existed, clouding your judgment as to whether or not you should go.

Embracing the negative language in your life may affect your decision-making. You must listen to yourself. That voice should be the loudest one in your spirit, not the thoughts of every other person who had negative thoughts or opinions. Look at some of your closest associates, co-workers, family members, etc. who exhibit negative talk at a high level. Look at their body language, their natural disposition, their outlook on life. You would think that if you saw the world through their eyes, Armageddon was coming in 20 minutes. In their mind, they have that sinking feeling where something always bad is about to happen in their life. These people exhibit neither a positive spiritual nor positive mental outlook towards life, and it often shows. Think of some of the more famous celebrities on television when they give interviews. You do not have millions of viewers tuning into a daytime talk show to hear negative talk the entire show.

Studies show that negative energy weighs heavily in your mind and affects your overall health. Negative thoughts may magnify realities into false perceptions. Dwelling on the negative, or constantly anticipating the worse negates the positive aspects that occur in your daily life. Think of a concert that you wanted to see that have great seats and had a great time. After the show on the way home, a tire blows out, and you are stuck on the side of the road waiting for 30-45 minutes for roadside assistance to come. A person with a more negative mindset will continue to dwell on the blown tire and feel that experience "ruined" his or her night. A person with a more positive mindset may be upset that it happened, but does not reflect too heavily as the concert should be the highlight of the night.

Attempting to achieve positive mental energy does not mean that you will have sunny days everyday. Everyone will have their moments when it feels that everything is working against them. For most, it is not possible to wake up every day and feel sunny and rosy inside. There is nothing wrong with that. The key is that you do not let them down days take control of your life. Do not let that negative energy bring you down, and find small victories somewhere. Your days are simple reminders that some positive energy and events are happening. The key is that you train your mind and spirit to learn how to seek and embrace that positive energy.

Possessing positivity is a habit that is contagious only if you dedicate yourself to engage in this fulfilling behavior on a consistent basis. Every day will not be full of the sunshine and euphoric thoughts. It is inevitable to encounter an event or situation that will challenge your overall Mental Fit. Developing a positive mindset helps you physically and mentally by lowering stress; decreasing the likelihood of depression; improved psychological and physical well-being; and better coping skills when encountered with stress[3].

---

3 "Positive Thinking: Stop negative self-talk to reduce stress." Mayo Clinic Staff; http://www.mayoclinic.org/healthy-lifestyle/stress-management/in-depth/positive-thinking/art-20043950

You and only you can take charge of your mental and spiritual energy. Despite the other influences that exist in your environment, you must find the inner strength within to thwart the wave of negativity, despair, and stress overload. To embrace the feelings of helplessness and hopelessness will not get you out of your situation. Continue to press ahead even during the darkest of times. You will be amazed of how much stronger you become and more resolute when you overcome adversity. The accomplishments that you experienced had some level of difficulty. To reach that level of achievement, you had to be strong and press forward, even though deep down or those surrounding you may make you feel otherwise.

Remember the road to blocking your success is you. Remove the stressors in your life. The funny thing about the stressors in our life is that we are highly aware of who or what the stressors are. The unfortunate thing is that we resort ourselves to levels of complacency and continue to let those that exist in our external environment continue to block us from our blessings. We should not resort to blaming our environment for some of the situations that we encounter. We should be able to look at ourselves and say that we led ourselves on this path where our flashpoint decision-making created some of the circumstances that we faced.

Negative energy may also come in the form of distractions. I think about the road I took in pursuing my career aspirations. I remember one year when I had allowed distraction after distraction persists in preventing me in my life plan. The people and events that caused those distractions may not be aware that I had deemed them distractions, but their energy sapped me from doing what I had to do. It is easy to get distracted to move away from our life's destined prize. I found introspective during the year of 2014 in understanding that if I continued to lose sight towards my accomplishments, I would continue to live in that proverbial box. As a result, I had to make some personal changes, and adapt to the core concepts of the Four Fits and speak them into reality. These personal experiences help shape the foundation of the book and the exercises that you see improved my personal self-development. I hope that these exercises will assist you in your life's path to your destination of success.

The next exercise included in this book includes a look into a moment of self-reflection. The goal of this exercise is for you to imagine that your life is the vehicle, and you are about to begin the journey of life. As stated before, roadblocks and other obstacles already exist in your life. Other unanticipated obstacles that you may not have prepared for pops up and test your resolve. The strength of your spirit and your inner being is to learn how to navigate through these obstacles and keep yourself intact.

Similar to thinking about your goals for the next 12 months, this exercise should force you to think about yourself and your surrounding environment. What is the source of your negative energy? What external forces exist that prevents you from becoming a better-rounded individual? The negative energy that surrounds you in your life, no matter how optimistic you are as a person, can bring you down, and affect you whether you are aware of this consciously or subconsciously.

You should adopt a practice of not blaming others for the situations in your life. Remember, we allow those who have negative influences or situations in our lives. Yes, we are born into certain environments. Some are born into poverty, single parent homes, living with grandparents, etc. However, we control our destiny. I will continue to state this throughout the book for you to say it and believe it. You control your destiny. When you grow to become a certain age, you should be able to take matters into your hands. Personal responsibility and accountability are trademarked traits for those who are successful in life. Take a step back and look at your local pastor, community leader, your favorite sports icon, or celebrity personality. They came from different backgrounds and had different stories of survival and overcoming adversity. Eliminating distractions and negative energy are keys to empowering you to become a leader and an inspiration to others.

Complete Worksheet #3 with this in mind. Ask yourself, what type of person you desire to become. Before becoming this person, you cannot be afraid to look at yourself internally. You must be able to look in the mirror and be proud of who you are as a person inside and out. If there is something that you may not like, you have the strength to change the appearance you see in the mirror. Remember, as long as you have life in your lungs, you should continue to strive for your level of greatness.

Identifying the negative "hotspots" in your life is a critical test under the Spiritual/Mental Fit. By recognizing the things in your life that ail you, you will develop a plan to address them systematically. Change does not happen overnight; however, change occurs when you recognize what needs adjustments. To make those changes in your life, you should not be afraid to confront the truths that lie before you.

As the goal for this exercise and this entire book is to develop, maintain, and nurture a positive mindset, obsessing over the negative is not the intent. The key is to become more self-aware and understand what in life challenges you, and what in life is presenting roadblocks on your path to success. There are some hard truths everyone must accept to overcome adversity. Some may experience it earlier in life than others. What you must keep in mind is that you are more than capable of overcoming those hurdles. Countless stories exist about those who may have lost a limb in war or due to poor health, lost their job, was in prison, homeless, etc., who overcame their looming hurdles to become successful in ways that they may not have had imagined during their predicament.

Everyone you see before you that have a success story met with obstacles at some point. Many people heard that they were not smart enough or good enough. Many people heard that they would amount to nothing in life. Some had their dreams mocked and laughed at in their faces. They found that inner strength to keep pushing forward. I draw inspiration from these people, even those I do not know. To this day, I still am in awe of how people overcame adversity to move forward. Like you, I strive to achieve the ability to continue to push past adversity and "bad luck." I ask that you continue to join others and me before us in embracing this same journey.

Once you have identified the negative energy that surrounds your life, you have laid the foundation for the Spiritual/Mental fit. A foundation is critical in adding additional pieces and building blocks in your life to continue towards your march to success. Being afraid or doubting yourself is normal. Even those who are the most successful in their careers and profession have had doubts. If you were able to ask them today, I am quite certain that some still harbor many misgivings, but have the resolve to press forward. What we will do together in this book is to find a way to identify where your resolve will come from, and how you utilize that to press forward with a purpose, plan, and vision.

Axiom #5: Turn your dreams into a vision, and make it a reality.

We are all dreamers of some way, shape, and fashion. We have dreamed for as long as we can remember. We often spend time dreaming about what our future may be. We have dreamed about whom we will marry, where we will live, our vacation, homes, and other opportunities that may exist. How many times do we find ourselves drifting off while at work, in a car, or gazing out the window? We ask ourselves what our dreams represent. We dream so often about the things that we desire in life, sometimes desperately to obtain those things by significant sacrifices.

As a child, the majority of us heard that we could be whatever we dreamed of being. For those who have young children, we tell them mostly the same thing. Although there are some truths to it, why is it when we are adults, we do not take this to heart? What has prevented us in achieving our dreams? The answer I would expect to hear if you asked most people is that life got in the way. Life is inevitable. A small fortunate few are what we consider lucky. The question we should ask ourselves is it truly luck or is it something more? More often than not, the answer is no. Life does not guarantee much of anything. Life promises adversity, hard times, unexpected losses, tragedy, surprises, and numerous twists and turns. Our lives are not scripted by what we thought it might be when you were nine or ten, playing on the playground, looking at the skies and dreaming what our lives will become.

Despite this sobering fact, we do not have to live in a world of woe is me. We often say at a certain point in our life is that in other life, we could have been this or that. Rather than accept this fatalistic line of thinking, we should look at life as a great challenge that we will conquer and overcome. Note, how I mentioned the words conquer and overcome. You will encounter some things that we cannot control. However, there are other tangibles and intangibles that we should influence, change the tempo, and outcomes of what our life may be. As stated several times before, we control our destiny and our life's path.

Rather than cringe or coil when faced with adversity, we should celebrate the challenges that we face and use the strength of our spirit and mental resolve to overcome the obstacles that face us. Find that inner strength deep down inside. If you are a religious person, tap into that strength deep down inside. Something to keep in mind in developing the Spiritual/Mental Fit is that the strength and test of your character lie within your ability to overcome adversity. You are not aware of your power when things are flowing well. Sometimes when things are flowing well in life, we are disillusioned about ourselves and ill-prepared for adversity at times. Those who are successful in life, and we are not talking about financially or academically, are capable to quickly develop ways to overcome adversity or be prepared when adversity hits.

There is nothing wrong with dreaming. I would imagine that everyone continues to dream up to the later stages of life. The key is to understand is that what you are dreaming about, and what does your dream mean to you for your overall sense of well-being and happiness. I continue to dream, maybe not as often as I used to; however, I still dream about what I can do, what I am, and what I will continue to strive to become. Yes, you should dream about what you should strive to be. Lose sight of that, and you will find that achieving what you are dreaming about will become marked with difficulty, adversity, and severe headaches.

Dreams may or may not have linear meaning. Often, they are subject to what is in your subconscious, your wants, and innermost desires. Dreams cannot come true unless you decide to do something actively to make them a reality. To make it a reality requires energy, and that energy does not exist within a dream. To make a dream into a reality, you must learn how to make your dream into a vision. There is a difference between dreams and visions. In dreams, your mind drifts to another place and time. As time elapses, some of the core components of your dreams disappear, or fades away. When you dream, you may remember the most vivid accounts of what happened or where you were; however, you may happen to forget or omit the smaller details. When you dream, you remember the most vivid accounts of what happened. In your vision, you construct everything together into a known reality.

Your vision should be the manifestation of your dreams. When you are dreaming of a new house, you visualize yourself walking up and opening the door, and seeing all you want in your new home. When you have this type of dream, you do not see the small, minute details as to what you experienced to see that dream come true. Dreams are vivid and full of your mind's eye may wish to see. In reality, to make those dreams come true, you must take that dream and construct it into a vision.

Having a vision does not mean that you lack that vividness that you had in your dreams. Your vision means that you are eyes are wide open. You can take what you seek and desire in life and attempt to shape it into a reality. Imagine the first true vacation you may have had as an adult. More than likely, you packed up and took off on your trip without much planning or an idea of what you truly wanted to do. Instead, you may have found yourself not maximizing your time, or feeling that you may have forgotten to do something, thus giving you a feeling of anxiety. Years later, when you are more of a travel veteran, you have the trip planning to an exact science down to how to pack, scouting out activities and restaurants, and other main attractions to see down to a nice, affordable budget.

Your vision provides your clarity and substance to what you have dreamed. I do not wish to discourage you from your dreams. However, I do encourage you to take your dreams and pursue them by converting them to a vision. Channel that energy and passion you may have had in your dream and make that vision as colorful and lively. Although I do not seek to make this axiom business-like, you should consider investing heavily in your vision and find a way to make it work. Speak it aloud to your closest friends, acquaintances, and family members who are supportive of you as a person. Remember to avoid the negative energy that could cloud your vision.

Therefore, I say to you, stop dreaming and go for your vision. If there are people who mock or does not understand you are a vision, forgive them for they are blind and lack clarity to see what you see. You must know that to get this axiom, you must understand the axiom before this concerning removing negative energy out of your life. If you continue to absorb the negativity that surrounds your spirit, it will be tough for you to overcome the roadblocks that you subconsciously placed within your mind.

The best-laid plans do not occur by being spontaneous. Spontaneity is helpful when faced with a quick decision you must make immediately. However, continuously being spontaneous is disastrous for your long-term success. Therefore, if you believe that by being spontaneous you will become successful, that is dangerous thinking. What you may not realize that being spontaneous is a good trait. This is especially true if you can hone this particular gift by being able to develop long-term thinking, and understanding the potentials risk and ramifications of your fast thinking and actions.

Remember that the only person that can define your success and destiny is you. Your definition of success will be different from the next ten people you would happen to ask their thoughts on this. Do not be preoccupied on what others may think may be successful. This is because their views are not likely aligned with yours. Furthermore, comparing your success and perceived challenges against another person is a not a health behavior. By making comparisons, you are not acutely aware as to what that person experienced to get to where they are today. As we do not follow them around 24/7, we are not privy to what sacrifices they made to get to the status where you may find yourself envious.

Someone who is making six-figures is considered from the outside as being successful, yet you are not sure as to the level of stress he or she is carrying to maintain that visual of success. Someone who is making $40-$50k a year may be successful because that person was able to achieve peace of mind, financial freedom, lack of health concerns related to stress and other disorders, and maintains healthy relationships with those in their circle. Similar to what the philosophy and mindset of the Four Fits are trying to achieve. I stress that you define your level of success and destiny as we are influenced, consciously or subconsciously, by what others are doing. As a result, we place undue pressure on ourselves to maintain a level of respectability by trying to live in what another person's definition of success may be.

The next worksheet will assist you in constructing your dreams into a vision. The first exercise consists of you being able to identify what dreams mean the most to you. You may recall the previous exercises throughout the Spiritual/Mental fit have focused on your list of twelve accomplishments and the immediate present. This particular set of exercises will have you decide what you wish to achieve or attain long term. To determine what you may desire for your future, it was important to review what you had accomplished in your past, and recognize what you are currently striving for in the immediate short-term.

Creating and maintaining a one, three-, and five-year plan provides you focus on what you are seeking to achieve. Unlike what we see on television, you are more than likely not able to catapult your life in a span of an hour or four weeks. Patience, faith, and perseverance are keys to sustaining your vision. If you continue to be overly distracted and impatient, you will easily stray off the path you created for yourself. Your one-, three-, five-year plans should be a testament to consistency, and developing your personal path to fulfillment in whatever areas that you seek in life. I challenge you to balance your plans with a mix of being bold, as well as having something safe to fall back on in the event you have to make adjustments.

Adjustments are keywords to consider anytime you are constructing your personal development. You will encounter some challenges that may temporarily halt your plans. If you are absorbed in your plans enough, your will and inner strength will help you veer back on the right path. Focus on areas that will improve yourself and your overall quality of life. Again, this journey is about you. This journey is not about your friends or family members, who may have a variety of opinions on what is best for you. Your plans should focus on connecting on all of the Four Fits, and you will see promising results.

Your plans should involve whatever makes you feel the most comfortable, along with touching on matters you may feel are important to you. You may want to buy a house for the first time or may be a homeowner seeking to move despite a lot of debt. In both of these situations, the more realistic option is to determine if moving fits into your one, three-, or five-year plans. If you have been completing your monthly 12 accomplishments, I would imagine that buying a home is not likely on the same list for most people. The reason being is that you may not have enough cash reserves or a suitable credit score to have a manageable house payment or home that meets some of the areas of your wish list. Placing a home as a target goal in your three- or five- year plan provides you with a more realistic chance of attaining some of your preferences.

One of the biggest mistakes we often make is that we feel, based on some sense of emotion, we should make purchases or feel that we have to have something right away. Even if we talk it up about being patient, we often consume our thoughts about whatever we are seeking would be or feel. This is the concept of dreaming. Again, there is nothing wrong with dreaming; however, dreams often involve a wide array of emotions. When you are creating your vision, you are turning your dream into a reality. The urge to have it right now is human. I have it often as well, and I must continually remind myself to stick to the script and stay on course.

Look at your list of goals you wish to accomplish in your 12 months. See if they align with your three- and five- year plans. If the answer is yes, continue to find ways to strengthen your knowledge and ease your spirit as you continue to drive forward. If the answer is no, do not be dismayed. Simply, think as to what you ultimately would like to accomplish in the future, and then plot down how you can make the incremental changes in the short run.

Being bold in setting your plans benefits you in several ways. It may help you break out of your shell or expand your line of thinking. Sometimes we are our worst enemy as we co-sign ourselves to complacency, or buying into the belief that this is how the way it is, and this is how it will be. Being bold may help steer you into a different career path, a different locale, new experiences, and increased self-awareness. Being bold and accomplishing what you set out to do creates a rewarding and exhilarating experience when you do accomplish what you had set yourself out to do three years later.

Setting your three- and five- year plans should not be stressful. If you find yourself stressing in trying to get to year three under the first year, you are doing more harm than good to your health and your self-esteem. Although I ask you to keep your goals and vision in mind as you continue to move forward, it should not be an object of obsession where you deprive yourself the right to life, laugh, and love. Referring to the list of 12 accomplishments you already have, you will recall that somewhere along the way, you were able to enjoy yourself a little along the way. Your vision should not be the source of stress or anxiety. To achieve your vision will take hard work; however, it should not consume every moment of your thoughts.

The beauty of the first set of worksheets under the Spiritual/Mental Fit is that you can see the seeds of your life placed in the ground to grow into something beautiful. You are responsible for nurturing, maintaining, and cultivating this Fit. Take each of these worksheets and staple them together, or place them in a folder or binder, and take the time to read and review what you put down over time. You will be amazed how you are slowly checking off all the essential items you addressed to develop a more holistic mindset, as well as connecting your mind and spirit.

Remember the five axioms under the Spiritual/Mental Fit. These axioms are more than just statements. They are rallying cries you may use to help keep yourself motivated. Do not be afraid to take a step back and reflect on what you have accomplished to date. Even if that accomplishment may be minor to another person, it could very well be vital to you. If that is the case, I implore you to nurture it. Embrace the talent, potential, and possibilities that lie within you and your world, and make it part of your life's destiny.

CHAPTER 3

THE EMOTIONAL FIT

YOUR EMOTIONS CAN be your biggest asset and your biggest liability. Regardless of how we attempt to present ourselves, we are all emotional creatures. The Emotional Fit is a fundamental component of the Four Fits. Holistic growth is something that comes from within. The best way to tap into that energy is to understand and utilize your emotions in a manner that is beneficial to you and your ongoing quest towards your personal development.

I presented this particular Fit second because it is closer in nature to the Spiritual/Mental Fit. Although the attempt to create the Four Fits is more of a sphere, wherein you can interchange each of the Four Fits into your interpersonal experiences, movement among the Fits does not require a sequential plan. For example, you may already be sound spiritually and mentally so you may focus more on the Emotional and Physical Fits. You may find yourself comfortable where you stand in three of the Four Fits. The beauty of this process is that you determine what areas are important for your life to develop, and you make the particular effort to enhance what you already have.

Enhancing what you have is a more compelling message to present versus changing yourself. We often equate our growth, maturity, and awareness of change. Although change is good, change can also be a generic way of looking at whatever may come to you in life, and you go with the flow without question or direction. Enhancing is taking that energy within you. Enhancing demonstrates what talents you have within you and nurturing it into something more definitive than what you likely did not know exist within yourself.

When you learned how to ride a bike as a child, you did not change yourself to learn how to ride. Realizing what you have within you and in front of you is stronger than attempting to become something else altogether. Realizing what you have within you and in front of you is stronger than trying to become something you are not. The power of what lies within you is waiting to be released. Understanding who you are and why goes a long way in your personal development.

Whether you are aware of this fact or not, your emotions are your guide. Some people are more emotional than others. Some people may not display any emotions at all when under duress. Those who do not display or feel that they rely on their feelings do not realize they use their feelings. It is because they do know how their emotions could impair their judgment when faced with adversity.

As we continue to work through the axioms and worksheets throughout the Emotional Fit chapter, you will want to ask yourself are you willing to look deep inside yourself and confront the truths that define you. Are you prepared to find a way to channel that energy into something bigger than what your mind imagined? Are you willing to recognize that you may have to dial it back as you continue to design your destiny? These are the questions that we should not only confront ourselves throughout this chapter but in our regular, day-to-day activities and interactions.

Often, we make hard decisions in our lives. Some are harder than others. Some may leave lasting scars and pain. I cannot even imagine or equate to some of the experiences of those I have encountered throughout my life. Some have gone through a hell that they do not wish on others. Their strength and way to overcome such adversity and still smile still amaze me to this day. Even though I may not have personally experienced some of the traumatic or serious life events that these people have confronted, I draw strength on their survival. Their views through the lens of my eyes provide me the inspiration to place the words in this book that you are reading.

People are heavily invested in their emotions when it comes to interpersonal relationships. Interpersonal skills involve family, co-workers, spouse, significant others, or casual acquaintances. What you must understand under the Emotional Fit is that your emotions are essential towards setting the tone of how you perceive the world and how the world perceives you. The overall focus of the Emotional Fit is to ensure that you continue to be aware of how you are feeling.

During the process of reining in your emotions, you become increasingly aware of your surroundings. Words spoken by another are easier to decipher. You learn how to step outside of your shoes while feeling the words spoken by another. Some people are capable of doing this naturally, while some may struggle while attempting to do so. Despite your perceived natural ability to be emphatic or not, you are more than capable of becoming conscientious of what you are feeling and why. You become cognitive of the meaning of words spoken to you by your significant other, your supervisor, or your friends.

Emotionally, you will see that your relationship with your significant other is a two-way street. The things that you desire and seek out in a relationship with another are determined by how you are as a person. Certain events, thoughts, and feelings that carry significant weight in your heart may negatively affect the ability to develop, nurture, and maintain a healthy relationship. By channeling the energy that you possess within yourself, you develop a sense of serenity, self-awareness, and empathy.

The axioms of the Emotional Fit cover different aspects. Some will cover relationship issues. Some will include your professional or interpersonal interactions with others. The purpose of these axioms is to show the diversity of emotions that lies within us, and how it may positively or negatively affect our lives, how we think, and how we operate in life. As stated before, these axioms are a foundation as you can create your axioms or something you can relate to as you operate within the Four Fits. These axioms are more of a beginner's guide in your journey towards a more holistic and balanced life.

Axiom #6: Do not let last past failings prevent you from future opportunities

In life, you will be disappointed. Everyone has experienced disappointments, some significant or severe one way or another. It is practically inevitable. Disappointments are painful and gut wrenching. The feeling of being let down after having your hopes up so high, and to watch it falter stings the spirit and soul. We have all been down this path. During the writing of this book, I continued to face disappointments. No matter how many times we set ourselves up to become optimistic, often it ends with the air sucked out of the room. When confronted with these moments, we sometimes revert to a fight or flight situation.

Giving up is very easy. You can stop reading this book right now, put it up, and never read it again. What is there to lose by not continuing to read this book? What is there to lose when faced with adversity, and you decide to go the other way to avoid confrontation or conflict within your spirit? What is there to gain when it hurts deep in your heart, and you often ask yourself, "Why bother, what is there to gain?"

Life is merely more than a game with many pieces presented to us during our lifetime. We are ultimately responsible for deciding the outcome of these situations. The choices we make, the words spoken from our mouths, the actions we make when confronted with a decision leaves a ripple that sometimes extends for years. A conversation that you had with someone two years ago may come back to your benefit or detriment two more years down the road. The beauty of life, despite all her cruel ways, is that we just do not know. Not knowing is what keeps us on our toes on a regular basis.

When everything is going easy and flowing smoothly, we sometimes develop a false sense of security. We tend to let our guard down and not be aware of what may pose as threats to us. When that happens, that false sense of security does not prepare as well for emergencies and situations where we must think and react quickly. For those who had a swift climb to success or moved around with ease, most do not react well when faced with adversity when it hits.

The challenges that confront us in life help create learning opportunities that create personal growth. If you learn from the experiences you encountered, whether good or bad, you gain an advantage over the next person by learning how to deal with a particular situation. This is similar to driving a car in bad weather for the first time. When traveling during a winter storm or a severe thunderstorm, it may have been nerve-wracking to you. You feel your heart beating at a 100 mph, and you felt like that you were never going to get past the ordeal. When you finally made it to your destination, you felt a sense of relief. When you encountered a similar weather event after experiencing it 20 times later, you may not even bat an eye. Gaining additional life experiences continue to provide you a gateway towards further personal development.

I recall a conversation that I had with a young woman who was struggling with her job. She had a hard time dealing with the criticism faced by her supervisor. She felt that she was not performing at a high level, and considered quitting. Her first impulse was to quit because when faced with adversity her natural response was to flee. When we discussed her situation, I encouraged her to step outside of her personal shoes and listen to her supervisor, rather than letting her emotions or experiences have her quit yet another job. By learning how to listen to the words said, she realized her supervisor was not personally attacking her; she was providing solid advice as she had the potential to go far with her company. The results were a promotion, renewed confidence, and a new set of lens to address her problems.

Fear of the unknown creates the response to flee, as it is easy. True inner strength comes from confronting your problems and past failings head on, learning from them, and growing to become a stronger person because of your response to your fear. Sometimes we may not have all the answers we sought when we faced with adversity. Sometimes the answer of why was confronted with this experience may not become known for years, but as the saying goes regardless of religion, everything happens for a reason. Our purpose is to seek an understanding and try to gain from our losses in the ways that we celebrate our wins.

Celebrating our wins has value to us. When we accomplish something that has significance, or won something in a contest, drawing, etc., we are elated. You experience a high from achieving whatever it was that you accomplished. For a couple of hours, days, or weeks, you feel like you are on top of the world. However, over the course of time, you will eventually slip back to a centered mind state. Elation is the exact opposite of despair and desperation. Although I am not saying that you should not enjoy the highs that come from an accomplishment, you must realize that it can be as fleeting as a loss.

The feelings are relatively different between a high and a low, which is true. What you must continue to do is to find a way to learn from both experiences rather than beating ourselves up from a high. If you completed your college degree you feel great, but what next? Can you continue to ride the wave of graduation and expect it to translate to immediate success? After the celebrations and relief, you eventually come to a realization that you must progress forward.

Take that same mentality from your perception of a failing or loss and use that same mindset to move you forward. If you happen to take a loss on anything, do not let that loss consume you. Do not let despair fester in you for more than 72 hours. Take three days to get it completely out the system. However, when you continue to fight through your despair, take the systematic steps towards fighting that despair and make it a learning experience that helps shape your destiny.

You control the energy that you allow into your spirit. As stated before, when you are around negative people, that negative energy enters into you whether you know this or not. Increased doubts and conflicted thoughts continue to grow in your mind rather than possessing mainly a positive "can do" attitude. The word "can't" pops up more and more because you slowly embraced that negative energy. The cloudy days look gloomier when you continue to maintain a negative demeanor within yourself.

To embrace and give into despair allows the other side wins. The other side is whatever you wish to define it to be; however, realize that side is not you. For the rest of our lives, we will continue to encounter something that will make us feel sad, despair, desperation, doubts, etc. It is almost inevitable. The key is to remember that you are pushing yourself to be successful in a manner that you seek to define success. Remember, the most successful people you see or associate as being successful finds that second gear to press forward during difficult times. Are they much different from you? The answer is no, but the difference is how they seek to overcome the obstacles that they face. You, too, will strive to overcome these barriers. The process may be complicated, but we can overcome it together.

Do not become envious or enamored with what others are doing around you. You can watch them from afar and admire their drive and determination. If you know them personally, do not be afraid to ask them for assistance or advice. Remember the whole premise of this book is to develop yourself holistically and learning how to live outside the box. Exposing yourself to different environments, people, and situations are an excellent way to add to your personal strengths.

We each contain core strengths that make us great. Some of us are more aware of our real talents than others are. Some are fortunate to learn and master them right away. Others may take years to develop, while the rest do not know what they truly have in their mind and hearts. Complacency should never be an embraced trait. Complacency brings about a sluggish mindset that may make you less motivated and less stimulated. I am not saying you should try to do something brand new every other month; however, you should find different things to keep you stimulated, and seek new challenges, no matter how large or small.

The next worksheet in this book (Worksheet #6) provides you an insight into what obstacles have stood in your way. Confront and embrace your adversity and turn those missed opportunities into strengths. When completing this worksheet, think of some of the events or occurrences that prevented you to becoming where you would like to be today or to-morrow. Reflect on the events that led to that event or occurrence, and reflect on how that made you feel.

This exercise may expose some old wounds. This exercise may recall some feelings of hurt. There is nothing wrong with going through these feelings again. Channel that energy and make it yours. Embrace that frustration and pain and use it to plant the seeds for a new future. Create a new destiny and continue to use that energy to nurture the new path that you are attempting to create.

As stated before, the most successful people would admit that they have a fear of failure or recalls a bitter experience where they considered it personally as a failure. They take that experience, and it helps them remain focused, or the fear of failing motivates them to do well. I cannot say that all people do this; however, that drive is something we are all capable of recreating within ourselves.

When I failed college the second time, it was easy for me to accept where I was in life and keep going. I had a job that had decent wages and decent benefits. I admit that at the age of 24, I was not the most responsible or goal-driven individual. That proverbial light switch did not come on because I focused my energies elsewhere, and it was mainly living to exist. The light switch came on by a couple of life-changing experiences. I had to face the realities of who I was as a person, and ask myself, is this the person that I wanted to be? Was this path the best route for me to help me achieve what I sought out the most in life? Were others truly to blame for the mistakes that I had made?

Arrogance is a fraction of confidence surrounded by the individual's many insecurities. Real confidence comes from knowing and embracing who you are, as well as your determination to make those areas of vulnerabilities into temples of strength. For those who we may see or know who portray a certain confidence about them, keep in mind they are fully aware of what makes them tick and what makes them weak. They know where their challenges lie within, but they continue to channel their inner strength and willpower to overcome them. Some challenges may take years to overcome, yet they keep grinding away. I wholly believe that every one of us is capable of overcoming most if not all challenges that we face. The key is having the right mindset and a changing of perspective to define what is your success.

Axiom #7: There is a difference between would like and want.

We often say to ourselves that we want this and we want that. Decades and generations ago, needs were paramount and wants were secondary. Change has occurred over time. Household dynamics changed. Different type of job opportunities and access to an array of financial resources are available more now than in the past. With that, our focus on our needs has shifted slowly towards wants.

I would like to say there is nothing wrong wanting something. The intent of this axiom is to change that mindset somewhat to focus on the bigger prize. Our wants often throw our emotions off kilter and ignore our needs. Sometimes, we become so emotionally invested into what we want; we miss what we need. Let us backtrack to the Spiritual/Mental Fit exercises to our list of accomplishments and our 12-month goals. The accomplishments are a mix of wants and needs; however, the common denominator for both examples is would like.

The phrase "would like" is a passive expression. Even though this book focuses on your overall personal development, being ultra-aggressive does not guarantee success. Taking risks is part of our human nature, as we all take risks. However, considering what you would like to have helps you take a step back and think what is that you truly seek, and what is it that you desire to have.

Determination exists when pursuing something that you strongly want and desire. The challenging thing about this particular balancing act is that if you allow your emotions to fuel what it is you strongly want, you could lose sight of the bigger picture. When seeking something that you would like to achieve or accomplish, continue to set your sights on the bigger picture. Avoid distractions and deterrence, but do not be afraid to self-evaluate and make the necessary adjustments to determine if pursuing your goal or objective should continue or table it for another day.

Life is a huge chessboard where you are always making moves with additional moves ahead. We experience numerous situations where we can make a decision that ends all dilemmas. Some choices made will create alternative situations and scenarios to consider. However, being able to recognize key moments in your life knowing that it may lead to more positive rewards rather than negative consequences should always be your end goal.

Every decision you make and every choice that you are presented will not result in a win. You will encounter some situations where you may chalk it up as a loss. How we interpret that loss is what continues our drive and hunger towards successful outcomes. Every successful person had encountered setbacks at some point in their lives. Some may have lost more than they gain over an extended time. The more they stumbled, the more they learned from the outcomes of their situation and eventually built upon their experience into a positive gain.

You may make an argument that to reach their end goal; they had to have a want. I would not argue against that because that is true. However, I am sure that in their decision-making process, they knew exactly what was acceptable to them and what was not. Thus, the rationale for the concept "would like" is a valuable tool in your personal development.

It is natural for us to become emotionally invested in something that has value to us, or something that we wish to have. The energy created by being emotionally invested helps us kick in gear to that next level that lies within us. If you have been active in sports at any point in your life, the energy you have by being emotionally invested into winning creates an adrenaline high in your efforts. Being emotionally invested provides us with some of our greatest highs when we attain a special accomplishment.

Being too emotionally invested into something can be considered unhealthy, and you encounter situations where you take risks that you normally would not consider taking. If you happened to become too emotionally invested in a relationship, you create a sense of dependency when you should be in a situation where you have two independent people creating a synergy amongst each other to fulfill each other's desires and needs. Unfortunately, being too emotionally invested creates poor mental energy that could lead to depression and, in some extreme circumstances, addiction.

Your mental health is critical in your personal development process. You will continue to face pitfalls. The key is not to succumb to them. Resist the temptation of wanting to give up (see the word "want"). Take a step back, breathe, and relax. When you engage the situation, engage it with the same amount of energy, confidence, and enthusiasm as you had when you first tried it. The main reason why most people give up and quit is not that they were not capable of doing what they set their mind to achieve. The main reason why is because their mental energy dwindled, and their enthusiasm and passion diminished. Therefore, find a way to re-energize yourself and go for what you would like to achieve.

In this era of technology, smartphones, demands of home/work life balance, and other obligations, the culmination of all these events become a drain on your mental energy. We have so much going on in our regular 24 hours that we often wish or felt that we needed another 12 hours to make the day worth it. Have you ever stopped and asked yourself why do we put ourselves through so much strain mentally and emotionally? I am quite confident that the majority of us could not come up with a reasonable answer. What you will likely respond with is an excuse of sorts or a long-winded explanation as to why we are doing what we have been doing for so long.

We regularly add so much to our plate when our main plate has yet to be clean. Similar to going to the buffet line and adding more food to your plate on top of the food that covers your entire plate, your mental eyes are bigger than your mental stomach. Gluttony of what you want can be as deadly as poor eating habits. Take your time and realize that we have a lifetime to achieve the things we seek to accomplish.

Recall your three- and five- year plans you completed under the Spiritual/Mental fit worksheets. The connection to the Spiritual/Mental fit to the Emotional Fit appears in this discussion as it relates to the conflict between your wants and would like. If you map out what you wish to accomplish in three or five years, you realize the charted a path to achieve what you are seeking. Yes, you may consider it as a want as you think about it at this moment. However, I am confident that as you continue to progress along the plans that you created, you may have made some smart, efficient, and necessary adjustments based on the reality of your situation rather than an impulse.

Worksheet #7 is a simple exercise of sorts. This activity should encourage you to think about what is it you want, and what would you like to have or be. In completing the exercise, you will notice there may be a small difference between the two lists. As stated before, there are similarities between wants and would like; yet, the goal is to understand what are you willing to achieve while understanding the pros and cons of your decisions.

Sometimes for us to achieve what we would like, we have to sacrifice the things we want most in life. When working on this particular worksheet, think of this more of an exercise of trade-offs. What are you willing to sacrifice or trade off to achieve something that you would like to accomplish or receive? Are you ready to strip away the blindness associated with wanting something bad enough so that you live in total peace and harmony within yourself? You must ask these questions yourself not necessarily in this worksheet, but even amongst some of the decisions, you must encounter in life. Search within yourself for those answers that path will open up for you.

If you ever played the game Solitaire on your tablet, smartphone, computer, or even with live cards, you are aware of what the actual objective of the game should be. After the first draw or draws, you see that you have limited options left to play out of the original deck. To build the four foundations up in ascending order, you scan to see what rows you can manipulate the cards to your favor. Life is set up in the same way. The Four Fits are set up the same way. You know where your suits are, but you have to maneuver around obstacles to line everything up. When completing this worksheet, try keeping this in mind. Sometimes we must search harder for the clues that lay before us rather than reshuffling the deck.

Once you can differentiate your ideal perception of wants and would like, you will slowly start to see how you can take more control of your destiny. You begin to strip yourself of what is a nagging emotion or thought in your mind to pursue something where your conscious does not hinder you from achieving that goal. Being emotional is a beautiful element to our overall personality. Some are more emotional than others; however, we must learn how to keep our emotions in check. If we allow our emotions to get too high or too low, we lose focus. This leads us to the next axiom.

Axiom #8: Do not let your emotions get in the way in making a business decision.

It is my hope that you see a consistent theme discussed throughout this book. The central driving element in completing the Four Fits is you. Although you have read seven axioms so far, the common thread that weaves this tapestry together is your ability to create a balance amongst yourself in four key areas that help determine the path of life that you elect to take. I am an emotional person. My emotions have empowered me to have a sense of empathy and belonging to something bigger than myself. I write this book with a passion for sharing my thoughts and feelings to those who are seeking some form of direction in his or her life. However, I realized that if left unchecked, emotions could lead to irrational and sometimes poor decisions in some of the choices that we make.

I am not asking you to turn your emotions completely off and become a cold-blooded robot that has no feelings or remorse. Instead, it is the understanding of your emotions and knowing when to tap into them, and knowing when to push them to the side to focus on your needs. By asking yourself not to be wrapped in your emotions while making a business decision, you are embracing a concept that will hopefully improve your decision-making. Hopefully, this will avoid some of the second-guessing we experience throughout our lives.

Think of a situation where your emotions got in the way of a decision you elected to make, and you regretted or felt that you should have made a different decision. It happens to all of us. Our emotions, no matter how engaged we are with them or not, are one of the central pieces of our core composition. When we are upset or angry, we tend to lash out and say or do the things that we normally would not do. When we are on a high of sorts, we tend to have our heads in the clouds, often missing some critical context clues that exist around our environment. If you are too emotionally involved, you do not notice the warning cues that may exist in the workplace, amongst our friends, or even purchasing something that we want rather than what we would like.

The beauty of our emotions is that they should continue to define who you are as a person. If you are an individual who possesses a high degree of empathy, you feel the pain and sorrow of others more often. You tend to care more about a situation to than others who may decide to look the other way. You may find yourself more engaged in circumstances and causes that align to how you identify yourself as a person. Being emotional is not a negative; however, being too emotional could be detrimental to your overall personal development.

Think of a situation where you based your trust in another person based on emotions. How often have you had a conversation with a friend, or even recognized yourself, about a situation where an acquaintance is going through a terrible situation and is asking for your assistance financially or through some other means. Because of the goodness that is in your heart, you tend to help your acquaintance without preconditions.

Whatever you extend to your relationship, he or she takes advantage of it, and you are now feeling upset, betrayed, or angry. Despite being helpful to those in need, sometimes there are those who take advantage of others who are emotional or too empathetic to another person's situation.

Although I am not advocating being an all-around Grinch, balance is the order that we should seek to take. Being keenly aware of your surroundings, external and internal, goes a long way in protecting yourself from making a poor decision. By taking the time to understand the gravity of your decision-making helps create the first several steps towards emotional independence.

Once we are adults, we encounter no other alternative than making decisions that could influence the rest of our lives. Some decisions may not be as earth-shattering as others; however, they do have an effect in areas and events that exist in our lives. If you recall the concept of looking at our decisions as flashpoints and crossroads in our lives, our decision-making is one of the primary drivers of what direction of the road we will take. If we allow our emotions to influence our decision heavily, you will often find yourself with some form of buyer's remorse, regret, frustration, and a lot of "why me."

When you first look at this axiom, you may think that this only affects major purchases. You may also believe that you should quit your current job. This type of decision-making extends to most facets of your life where you must make a decision that, whether you know this or not, may be a critical decision in your life. The majority of the decisions that you choose to make should have a business-like mentality only in the event that you know that it may affect something in your life later on down the road. If you are deciding what to eat, or where to go for vacation, that is not a life-altering moment. However, traveling somewhere knowing that you have a full-fledged hurricane that may hit the beaches because that is what you had your heart set on for that weekend is making a decision with your emotions so heavily involved.

Your decision-making at work can be negatively affected by your emotions if they are not balanced. You may have a co-worker that you do not like, you are his or her supervisor, and those feelings are evident in dealing with this individual. For every time your employee makes a comment or brings something to you, you are quick to lash out or say something construed as negative. By the time you attempt to change that aspect of your personality, your previous actions as displayed to others, make you appear to be the disruptive individual. That does not mean I am advocating being something that you are not; however, the fact that you allow your emotions to affect your relationship with your employees or coworkers negatively influenced how you two could work together.

I recall a conversation that I had with a young woman who had a lot of potential and upside, but she was very raw in her personality. Rather than focus on her overall potential and growth, the politics and the conflict that resided within the office consumed her thought process. It is apparent that her perceived adversaries do not have her best interest at heart. However, rather than engaging those who provide conflict to her, removing the emotions would have been the best course of action. The words and actions uttered by another person can affect you only if you allow it.

For example, you meet another person that you are interested in and start dating. Initially, the exchange between you and the other person is cordial. As time goes on, the feelings intensify. The words and actions from your mate begin to affect you more than it did in the past. Why is that? You become more emotionally invested in the relationship that you have with your mate. If the same words came from another person, you would more likely than not ignore or dismiss the comments and actions of what another person may do because it did not personally affect you. Now, as you have become emotionally invested, the words and actions intensified, sometimes resulting in wrong interpretations.

Worksheet #8 provides you an opportunity to examine where you faced a situation or an encounter where your emotions may have gotten the best of you. During this ongoing process of your personal self-development in this book, I will encourage you to remove the negative thoughts associated with regrets. We all make mistakes in life. It is almost inevitable. We do not have all the answers to every situation, event, or scenario we encounter. Rather than looking back and using a word with such negative connotation as regret, look at it as a learning experience in life.

Recall the example of driving a car. From your teenage years to adult life, you logged a countless number of hours on the road. You have likely driven through numerous weather experiences, traffic jams, or limited visibility. The more experience you gain by these events, the more confidence that you build for future encounters. Your life experiences are of the same mindset. You may have overcompensated on a slick road the first couple of times, but the next several occasions after that, you feel more confident about how you should maneuver the road.

This exercise is segmented in three ways for five situations you encountered that you knew that your emotions got in the way of making a sound and practical decision. These three sections are helpful by having you look at the past and understanding not only what happened but also why did it happen. You may select a broad range of experiences for this exercise, as this exercise involves you. I ask that when completing the exercise, you refrain from using relationship situations. We will address that later in the book.

The first segment addresses the situation in itself. As with other exercises thus far, do not be afraid, to be honest with yourself. To grow holistically, you must develop a general sense of being honest with yourself, and demonstrate the desire to improve yourself in all four phases. Honesty during this process helps the healing process and create areas of improvement where challenges currently exist.

The second segment addresses the emotions you experienced and how did you deal with that situation. Think closely about not only the situation itself but also how it may have possibly affected others around you. Remember that you are a thread within life's tapestry. Others will come and go, and others will stay in this tapestry as you deem fit. You will regularly make decisions as to the importance and value of the relationships you establish with others. Thus, to complete this exercise, you must develop an ability to step into another person's shoes and do this flawlessly.

To step in another's shoes or see things through their lenses is difficult to do at first. You have to be honest and have humility amongst yourself first. We all have our biases, opinions, and quirks; however, when we interact with other people, ask yourself how others view you through their lens. What image are you trying to portray? You should not have to do wholesale changes to appease another person. However, to be able to control the tone, pace, and tempo of your relationships by providing a holistic balance helps expands your consciousness to the bigger picture.

The actions and words of another can have an impact on your world, whether positive or negative, by the means that we allow them to affect you. The reverse also applies by the actions and words you put on display towards others. Whether you are at work, school, at a social event, or family gathering, I encourage you to take a step back and carefully examine the words you said, or how you had responded to a conversation or situation, and ask yourself, is there something that you could have done differently.

The third segment of this exercise provides a response to what you recommend for yourself on how to proceed when faced with a similar situation. During the self-evaluation process during your personal development journey, often step back and provide yourself recommendations on what is best for you and those around you involved in each scenario or encounter. The question you should ask yourself during the self-evaluation process is "how do I rate myself?" Again, this is an exercise in honesty and humility. Once you demonstrate how you are capable of doing this in a consistent fashion, you will find the decisions to become more fluid and aligned with more confidence.

Seeking another opinion on your life is not your opinion. I can provide numerous illustrations about what may work for you or how you should address virtually every situation; however, my opinion derives from my life experiences. I know myself and am comfortable within myself to understand the how and why of my words and actions; however, what worked best for me may not personally work for you. The Four Fits is a guide and a template, but you are free to create your version of axioms and create your personal worksheets. This book merely provides a roadmap about the direction you choose to take on your journey towards your personal development and your destiny.

Incorporating another person's opinion entirely without providing any insight from your perspective is detrimental for your overall growth. The more opinions you seek on how to proceed creates an interdependency that is unhealthy for you mentally and spiritually. Being interdependent is part of our lives and our world. We all rely on something from somebody, somehow, somewhere. From the food you eat to the lights that turn on in your home, to the gas you need to drive your vehicle, we live in a world of complete interdependence. However, this goes back to the axiom of the wants vs. would like vs. needs. We should continue to stay away from that "wanting" mentality as we sacrifice a part of ourselves in the process. You cannot be holistic if you continue to give yourself essential parts of your personality to attain the things that you want. Seeking the answers for you, and within you, comes from developing an ability to connect spiritually and emotionally.

Axiom #9: Take time to know yourself, and love yourself

Throughout this point, you were introduced to various ways to develop yourself spiritually, mentally, and emotionally. The next two axioms will address your emotional self from within. The reason why this path existed in this fashion was to place checkpoints in your life that you feel comfortable mapping out and following through. Each exercise up to this point had a variety of ways that helps you look at yourself in the mirror and evaluate the type of progression that you made before taking this journey.

As stated under one of the previous axioms, the road to blocking your success is you. Your definition of success will be different from the next person and so on. The purpose of this overall personal development process is for you to define your success in the manner that best fits your purpose and vision. The checkpoints you created by mapping out your one, three and five-year plans contribute to creating a path towards achieving your goals. Understanding that differences between what you want and would like helps you make decisions that align to what fits best for you

Before we continue to move to the next axiom, take a step back and look at the worksheets that you have worked on from the beginning. Look at the progress you made! That person is you transferring your energy, thoughts, and passion into something concrete and tangible. Being able to look back at your vision is similar to looking back at pictures that you took of some momentous occasion or a random snapshot while out with friends and family. We can conjure up memories of what happened back then from time to time, especially when it leaves a lasting footprint in your mind. When you see a picture from yesteryear that brings up stronger memories and conversations of what was going on at that moment. Leaving a written "photograph" of what you have accomplished or planning to achieve will also bring some desire to push forward or a sense of pride in the work you put into yourself.

You must believe in yourself. Even though we all are accustomed to having a support system, you are responsible for yourself. You cannot complete the Four Fits process until you can look at yourself and embrace who you are, and where you have been. You may come from a hard life wrought with adversity, pain, heartache, and tears. You may come from a privileged background, or from a supportive family dynamic; however, it is not where you started from, it is where you finish. Those experiences should enlighten you because they help shaped who you are as a person inside and out.

Live your life without regrets. For every action taken and for every word uttered, keep in mind that there is a resulting action. In our daily activities, there is a perpetual cause and effect in motion. For the moves that you made in the past, you can see the connecting dots to what shapes your experiences, bias, perceptions, and your version of reality. The people we meet or continue to meet serve different purposes in our lives. It is up to us to determine how that person, place, or event fits into our world.

Despite the determination you have towards your path to success, you must take time out for you. When I speak to others about the stressors that are in their life or how busy they are, I often ask this a simple question, "What is something that you like to do?" The majority of the time, the answers involves something to do with another person. As stated before, a heavy dose of interdependency impedes our future growth and development. Even if you are in a dating or marital relationship, you must find the time to do for yourself, and not for others.

We have different jobs, careers, responsibilities, and obligations that take up a lot of our time on a regular basis. However, we must learn how to unplug ourselves from these realities or the level of stress and likelihood of burning out increases. You have to ask yourself, how is it possible for you to achieve what are you seeking to gain when there is nothing left in the tank for you to enjoy it? Does obsessing over everything solve your problems right away? Does consistently engaging headlong into a confrontation or a disagreement provide the results that you need?

Even if you have a strong-willed personality, there is nothing wrong being passive and deferential to life at times. Let us recall earlier the discussion about building a house from the ground up. No matter how much money, resources, or personnel that you have dedicated to it, it is virtually impossible to have a home erected in one day. Many moving parts are in play, with people that have different skill sets that must do their part to complete building your house. If you rush too quickly to erect the house, there will be serious flaws with the design which costs you in the long run by attempting to fix those flaws. Life is similar in that you do not take the time to do for yourself, heal your mind and your spirit, you will expend additional energy into cleaning up whatever errors that you made.

So many times, I hear about the grind people undertake to provide better opportunities and outcomes. The question begs itself; however, once you accomplished what you set out to achieve, how will you be able to enjoy it if you burned yourself out in the process? What about the physical and emotional strain you place on your body and mind, and to some degree, leaves long-lasting scars? You must take the time out of your busy schedule and all the activities and find time to take care yourself in all areas, or the sacrifices you made to date would all be for naught.

The cascading effect from pushing yourself so hard is that you struggle with learning how to let go. If you were not OCD before, you would likely become OCD now. This new personality trait occurs because you are hell bent and determined to overcome adversity and hard times that when you do reach a level of success you defined months or years ago, you continue to push mentally even harder than when you originally started. You push and push until you lose the identity of yourself, and when you lose the identity of yourself, a piece of you is lost and stored away in the recesses of your spirit.

Sometimes you become so engrossed in a concept, idea, or a vision that you tend to forget what brought you to the point to move forward. Sometimes you become your harshest critic, constantly looking at flaws and perceived failures of what you are doing to the point that you easily overlook what you have accomplished. It is easy to do. I hope you have completed or referred to the worksheets provided up to this axiom. These worksheets provide not only a template for driving your success but a reminder of the successes that you already achieved!

Worksheet #9 is different from the previous eight worksheets. The purpose of this worksheet is to provide you a cooldown from the intensity of the efforts you put in place up to this point. You cannot live or feel free when you continue to enslave yourself to something that you do not have complete control or something that you cannot change right away. If you are saving for a new car or house, you will not have the money overnight. If you are traveling to a particular destination for vacation, the trip will take time no matter what method of transportation you select.

To complete this worksheet, you will need to take a personal inventory of your place of peace and serenity. For every line you attempt to complete, ask yourself this question, "Does this provide me a peace of mind, and does this take me to a place towards serenity?" Find a hobby or a passion you enjoy, or you may feel you could enjoy and make sure you incorporate that into your routine. Designate some time for you to take that step back and enjoy yourself.

Whatever you ultimately decide to do to enjoy yourself, I recommend that you remove yourself from the environment that currently gives you the most stress or is the source of your current level of stress. If you are working on a project at work, finding a hobby or something to relieve some of the stress at the same location does not truly provide benefits for your well-being. You consciously and subconsciously pick up visual and audio cues that alert you to your surroundings. If you continue to surround yourself with the same reminders, your mind will inadvertently start to slip back into work mode.

When I was in school, I made sure that I dedicated myself to doing my homework, research, and writing at a particular time of the day. Even though I was not and still sometimes cannot be the most regimented of people, I realized that if I dedicated a set time to focus on that aspect of my life, my focus improved. I realized that during that time I was able to focus on myself, I did not feel as much pressure to focus on school. Of course, there were times when my routine was off from time to time, but I did dedicate myself to stick to a particular schedule.

Life will continue to go on if you decide to take a break for yourself. The best-laid plans of your vision and the path of success that you are trying to create for yourself will still be there if you took a step away for a short period. The mind, body, and spirit can only withstand so much. You are not a machine no matter how determined you are to make things work. You cannot fix what ails your situation if you do not learn how to take the time out to fix yourself emotionally and mentally.

A mental reprieve from the energy you have put out is beneficial in several ways. First, it takes away the pressure that builds up from within. When you are fatigued physically and mentally, you tend to have mental errors. Your concentration and memory will not be as sharp as if you were refreshed. Depending on the type of work you perform, you put yourself and others at risk. By taking the time out to recharge your batteries, you will feel more re-energized to address your issues and vision with a fresh slate.

The second reason why taking a mental reprieve is beneficial for you is that the world needs you. It may sound a little ironic saying to take a step back and then engage the world; however, the world has so much to offer. Find something new and adventurous to do. By exposing yourself to something new and different, you will find yourself pulling away from whatever that ails you. You overwhelm your senses by breaking the repetition that you have set for yourself for your routine. It is relatively easy to get up, get dressed, go to work, go home, and attend to whatever requires your attention at some point and fashion. I challenge you to try a different route to take home from time to time. Go somewhere different along the way and be anonymous amongst the crowd. Sometimes the unknown creates an inner sense of excitement that stimulates your mind again.

The third reason is that pushing the envelope does nothing more than tearing the envelope itself. Finding inner peace and relaxation ensures that it keeps the content of your envelope together. When you drop that piece of mail in the mailbox, you guarantee that whatever you placed in that envelope or package will reach its destination in one piece. Your mind is similar to that envelope or package. You do not want to come apart, become ruined through mishandling, or exposing it to something that makes the envelope loses its sturdiness. Keep the contents of the envelope together by keeping the contents of who you are as a person together despite what you are pursuing, and going out your way to preserve one of the most precious gifts you have, which is your mind.

Axiom #10: Your love resume should be filled with as many accomplishments as your work resume

Relationships are tricky. Relationships can be complicated. When we were in high school or our early twenties, the majority of us had simple responsibilities and simple obligations. Life was not complicated with the nuances that plague the majority of our lives today. Our day-to-day activities allowed us to move more carefree and without many restrictions in our lives. Relationships today continue to meet as many challenges as those that exist in our individual lives.

One of the key fundamental things to remember when it comes to relationships is that it consists of two people agreeing to get together as one. If you seek to build something together, you must understand how that one operates as a single unit. Developing a fundamental understanding of each other is one piece of your relationship survival guide. A relationship consists of a total unit that cannot function without the balance created by two separate parts.

Similar to the saying that no two snowflakes are identical, your relationship fits that same philosophy. There are similarities in relationships; however, both parties involved define the scope, nature, and direction of the relationship. The moment that you allow others to dictate any of the three areas above, your relationship slowly enters into a perilous situation Allowing others into your relationship creates noise that could not be healthy.

Because we are now in a world where information and the speed of thought and communication have increased exponentially, we should be mindful as to the information we share with others about your relationship. Although you may be a relatively private person or a person who may not be involved in much gossip, the feedback you may receive could create more strains into your relationship. Conversely, the opinions received by others may have no significance to your relationship because there are two sides to every story. When a couple goes to therapy, they work on their problems together with a neutral party. When we often discussed our problems in our relationship, that the other party is not there which makes the conversation slanted and heavily one-sided even if you are accepting of your challenges.

Being mired in negativity at work will follow you home no matter how strong-willed you may be. If you allow that negative energy permeate into your being, you will carry that negative energy for an extended period even after you leave for the day. You cannot totally avoid negative people at work, as they are everywhere; however, you do not need to immerse yourself in that negativity. Removing yourself from the negativity allows your mind to focus. Furthermore, when you head out for the day or begin to discuss your day with your partner, that negative energy has dissipated, and you speak of it as a generality.

This particular axiom of the Emotional Fit is appropriate for anyone whether you are currently in a relationship or seeking to be in one. This particular axiom does not provide a specific blueprint for fixing or saving a relationship. However, if you are looking to improve yourself by creating your personal development plan, you must keep in mind how your new sense of direction affects others that are in your life. Relationships, in particular, experience challenges in survival if left unattended.

Like the previous axiom involving taking the time out to do for yourself, you should also save some of your extra energy into your relationship. Although you are sacrificing much energy for something greater, a relationship thrives on the energy that you give, as well as your partner. The challenge of relationships comes when one partner is so engrossed with their career or vision that they forget about the unit formed by their partner.

We pour an extensive amount of energy into our jobs. We spend the majority of our days and weeks at our jobs forging relationships with our co-workers, supervisors, and customers. We work to pay bills, entertainment, dining, among other responsibilities. It is almost inevitable that we must perform some work to meet our basic needs and to do some of the things we would like to do. Although that is a necessity, you must continue to work on areas outside of your professional or personal aspirations.

When we look for a new job, career, or seeking promotion, we are required to come up with a resume. When asked to come up with a resume, we sit and ponder what we have accomplished to date in a fashion that makes the resume looks presentable. We tend to go out of the way to find someone to help craft our resume by providing our job description and explaining what we do so we can have the certain keywords to be found in a search engine.

If we wrote our love resume, what would it say? If we presented this resume out in the market, what kind of "hits" would you receive? How can we market ourselves to our significant other? If you presented these questions to a group of people who are currently in a relationship, it would be interesting to see the responses provided.

We focus so much on defining ourselves for strangers that we often do not pay attention to our personal resume. We consume ourselves with appeasing another person to give us an opportunity that we often forget whom we need to please knows who we are, and is right around the corner. Sometimes we fail to realize how much we neglect our obligations with the one that we are in a relationship. This holds true in relationships where you are not intimately involved with another person, as it can apply to our interpersonal relationships with friends and loved ones.

The passion you seek in your personal growth and development should incorporate time for your loved ones. Even though you are trying to live a life free and without dependency, your interdependence on others is key to the vitality of your overall growth. You should always be considerate as to how your path may affect others. Being too immersed in your job without the appropriate support system in place adds to the stressors that come with your job, and it also affects your overall health and relationships.

When you have support emotionally and mentally from your partner, it allows you to let the wind sail beneath your wings. Being able to discuss your triumphs, challenges, and projects you are about to undertake provides an opportunity to improve communication. Do not allow the conversation to be one-sided, or to be an ongoing discussion of a fatalistic nature. I would also encourage you to avoid having a conversation about work every day. Allow time to discuss your day briefly, but do not make it appear to be an obsession.

In most relationships, opposites do attract. Your partner will likely have a different type of personality than you. Therefore, be mindful of your partner when discussing work. You may have a partner who elects not to discuss work because once the day is over, the day is over. Therefore, an extended conversation about work throughout the evening and into the night is something your partner does not necessarily want to hear but listens to be supportive. If you are in that situation, take the time to recognize that aspect about your partner, and limit how much time you dedicate to discussing what happened on the job.

Sometimes when you are discussing what happened at work, you may tend to become emotionally charged which has an adverse effect towards your partner and loved ones. Recall the previous axiom where we completed a worksheet that identified the stressors and what hobbies and activities that take your mind off those stressors. Dedicate that same energy to your relationship, as it will help you on those stressful days at the office.

For the next exercise under Worksheet #10, you will complete a resume with a twist to it. This exercise should be a light-hearted exercise that focuses on your creativity. Although the exercise is to be fun in nature, there is some seriousness involved with this exercise as you may recognize there are some areas you may need to improve on in your love life similar to how you try to seek improvement on your job skills.

Even after you complete this exercise, note that you can always come back and see what areas you have made an improvement over time, or notate areas that continue to need work. Even if your partner is not on the same or shared path towards his or her personal development and growth, your partner could benefit in filling out this worksheet as well. Do not be afraid, to be honest with yourself, similar to other exercises that you have completed previously. Communication is essential in any interpersonal relationships, including a relationship with your significant other. By completing this worksheet, a new set of dialog could be created which causes an improvement in your understanding of each other.

Do not be afraid to acknowledge the challenges that exist in your relationship. Sometimes that answers do not come right away. Working on those challenges on your end, and recognizing areas where you need to improve will benefit your partner tenfold. Assuming your partner is as vested into the relationship as you are, your partner will feed off the energy and likely follow your lead. Do not be discouraged about what you write down for this exercise. Remember that this whole book is a combination of personal reflection, joy, accomplishment, and adversity. If you are sincere about the philosophy of the Four Fits, you will be able to look at yourself in the mirror every day with a mindset that you will overcome any adversity because you were not afraid to look adversity in its eye.

The Emotional Fit encompasses different areas in your life from work, home, personal, and relationships. Your emotional health and stability play a vital role into your acceptance of the successes and setbacks that you will encounter in life. When confronted with challenges or adversity, it is easy to lose yourself in your emotions. There is nothing wrong being an emotional being; however, refuse to allow your emotions from getting in the way of thinking clearly. The energy you give out to become successful, based on your definition of success, will be draining at times. Despite this fact, you should allow yourself time to take care of yourself, remove yourself from stressors to tend to your mental well-being, as well as enjoy your time with your friends and loved ones.

CHAPTER 4

THE FINANCIAL FIT

THE FIRST TWO Fits focused on your mental and emotional state of mind. If you are following this process the first time through the book, you encountered some difficult decision making and confronting yourself with hard realities of where you currently are. I would like to tell you that it is ok to feel somewhat frustrated or challenged by coming up with some of the answers for the worksheets associated with the first two fits. This is a good thing because personal motivation/self-help books typically provide feel good stories and tell you that all in the world is rosy, when in actuality it is not. You must find it within yourself to design and create your destiny.

Even without incorporating some of the axioms found under both Fits, I ask you to challenge yourself and challenge yourself often. Your success is dependent on the energy generated from within yourself to transfer to your mind, body, spirit, and soul. The synergies produced in this circuitous loop help lift your spirits on your cloudiest of days, and provide you strength when you go through difficult times. Recall how that I relatively strayed away from the religious aspect of your development. This is due to the fact you must recognize that you are broken from within and working on that while developing your salvation. Through the process of your ongoing self-development, you will find a oneness within yourself. You will be more in tune with whatever your belief of a higher power is, and that connection will flow right through you as well.

Please keep in mind that as you are reading this, I am writing this from a perspective of someone who still has a significant amount of debt. I am still searching for that perfect fit for myself, and consider myself very flawed. I find that by sharing these concepts into a book and putting this on display to you, I envision a connection with each of you with a common purpose to provide improvement for a variety of reasons that we each hold dear. I currently am using these tools and reminding myself of these axioms. The byproduct during this incredible journey of providing a compass for your world is that I feel that complete and holistic connection with myself, and I hope you feel that connection with me. I do hope that by completing the worksheets and taking the time to absorb the words you are reading; you find that passion for redeveloping your vision in a way you feel is best fit.

One of the main reasons I provided the Spiritual/Mental and Emotional Fits to you first is that they are concepts of abstract thinking. To be an abstract thinker, you must be able to free yourself from the constraints that are holding you back. To be an abstract thinker, you must be able to see the world in different colors and hues. The next time when it is bright and sunny outside, stare up at the sky and what do you see? Even in the clearest of days, your eyes will see the birds, planes, and maybe some thin clouds high in the sky. If you are not thinking in an abstract manner, you will likely look up and say it is sunny and bright. Those words are devoid of meaning, and the interpretation is relatively bland.

The second reason for the initial design of the Fits is that by learning how to see and control your thoughts in an abstract fashion, seeing the world in a more linear and concrete fashion becomes easier. The movement and transition from one Fit to another when you first approach these worksheets involve a degree of discipline and humility. However, as you continue to move from one phase to another within each Fit, you can easily go back at any point and make the necessary improvements to your vision.

To develop a holistic thinking, remember to think yourself as a whole as in a circle or sphere. To live within that sphere of thinking, you must learn how to live within an ongoing blend of abstract and concrete thinking. Concrete thinking helps create the balance that you need to continue to develop your path towards success. To be able to see your destiny in a linear fashion means you are capable of staying on task for actionable items that may help push you over the finish line.

The next two Fits designed in this book focuses on the concrete, linear thinking. At this point, assuming that you have completed each worksheet before addressing these last two Fits, you have clarity into what you are doing and understanding the depths of why you are crafting your vision in a clear and meaningful fashion. The axioms for these last two Fits are shorter in length as they are more task-oriented in nature and require you to focus on your ability to stay on task by utilizing regular checklists throughout the process.

The Financial Fit focuses on areas where most of us everyday people struggle, which are our finances and financial security. The Financial Fit, similar to the other two Fits, does not provide a comprehensive strategy for financial independence. The Financial Fit does not show you how to become a millionaire overnight. That is because thousands of other books with that premise and the majority of those who do buy and commit to those books at some given point of time do not stick with the advice provided by those who have been successful. Also, at least from my vantage point, it is difficult to relate to the books, as everyone's situation is different. Each one of us has a different drive, personality traits, and levels of commitment. In this book, I am not asking much for you to do. In these next two Fits, the concepts are the same as they have been throughout the book.

As we tackle the Financial Fit, I ask that you please keep an open mind as I introduce more research and supportive information to provide a rationale as to why this will help ease your peace of mind. As stated throughout this book, you define your level of success as well as your destiny. Your commitment to this, along with the Physical Fit, is determined by your level of dedication and determination to succeed. As such, the axioms provided will again provide a template of key areas where the most ordinary people who live everyday lives are capable of completing. If you do become a millionaire in the process, I applaud your efforts. This leads us to the first axiom.

Axiom #11: You cannot be a true millionaire unless you learn how to be a "thousandaire."

Recall the numerous conversations that you have with friends and family about financial plans. Often you hear them say that their goal is to be a millionaire. If you happen to ask them how they are going to achieve this, some of the responses provided will amuse you. To reach the pinnacle of this financial milestone is not easy. To reach this milestone, you must develop a foundation.

One out of every sixteen households in this country feature millionaires[4]. The number of millionaires has grown by close to 20% over the last several years. The path these households take to get to this milestone varies from household to household, and from person to person. You must determine what is your best way to reach this milestone; however, you must have an understanding of how these individuals or households were able to get there.

The majority of millionaires do not live as lavish a lifestyle as you see in various media outlets and photos. The typical age of a millionaire is 62. That means that if you are in your 30s or 40s reading this book, you have more than enough time to reach this point, but it comes down to how savvy you are in managing your finances. For those who were able to reach that pinnacle, they were able to take a variety of measures from investing, cost-cutting, purchasing items of need and focusing on things that they would like. Recall the axiom concerning wants and would like. Even though the millionaire may have his or her sights on a particular purchase or investment, they are not motivated by taking risky behavior that drains his or her finances.

---

4 A Millionaire on nearly every block in U.S., Richard Morgan, http://nypost.com/2014/06/11/number-of-millionaire-households-in-us-rises-again/

To gain momentum of being a millionaire, you must be able to concentrate on the current investments you have today. Understanding how to utilize your finances by investing properly, identifying areas to trim your spending, making conscious decisions about when to particular a particular item, and the need for lowering debt. You can search anywhere on the Internet for books and articles about how to increase your finances, but it is important to have the baseline understanding of how your spending habits may affect your ability to be financially secure.

Being financially secure is a goal that many of us seek and desire; however, many of us are not sure as to how to do so. To focus on your Financial Fit, you must have the will, patience, and determination to become financially secure. I do not believe you have to be a hermit and live in a shell for the rest of your life. You can enjoy some of life's greater things to offer; however, you must have restraint. You must have a plan you can always go back on and see if you are reaching the critical goals of your financial path.

As stated before, you do not have to go to school to be educated. The same applies to financial principles. You do not have to have a finance, economics, or accounting degree. You do not have to be an MBA or a CPA. A vast amount of information exists in a variety of arenas for you to seek and attain the information and knowledge to improve your financial situation. I would encourage you to casually review articles on the internet, or even read the financial sections of newspapers as they have great investing and financial advice. You can learn about how to lower debt, develop a basic understanding of how financial markets work, or even understand how to manage your retirement plan.

Recall learning how to cook that meal or recipe that your mother or grandmother makes every year for Thanksgiving. You ask her for the recipe or how does she make it. More often than not, you will hear she got the basics from their mother or grandmother, and they added a little twist. Handling your personal finances follows that same formula. You can learn how to make a good hamburger in 100 ways, but after practicing it repeatedly, you taught yourself how to make that perfect burger for you to the point where others are asking, "Hey, how did you make that hamburger that tastes so good?"

The first key to moving to a thousandaire is to understand where you currently stand financially. Find out how much your net worth is. Do not be ashamed or discouraged if you have a negative net worth. As I am writing this book, I have a negative net worth myself. I have the mindset and attitude that I am confident of turning this around and making solid decisions to improve my net worth to be positive. You must understand your debt situation as well. It is relatively easy to get credit to the point where we drown in it. The question you should ask yourself is, do you understand how debt works against you? It is more than acknowledging that you have debt and you can afford your minimum payments, but understanding and despising debt is a mindset you should try to develop. I will provide an example for you to consider.

During a conversation that I had with another individual, we discussed how much debt we are carrying. During the conversation, this person informed me that she had approximately $43,000 in revolving credit card debt. She has several credit cards from the major credit cards to the retail cards. I asked her how much she is paying in minimum payments. She said that she is paying approximately $750 in minimum payments for her credit cards alone. These payments do not include mortgage, student loans, and a car note. I asked her how much she is paying in interest each month. She was not sure. I encouraged her to look at her statements and let me know. She informed me that she is paying approximately $520 in interest per month in credit card debt alone.

Now with the $520 that she is paying in interest, she has to understand that she is throwing away over $6,000 a year in interest. That $6,000 could be invested in other areas to improve her financial standing, or just have $6,000 in play money. That money could be used for her Christmas shopping, planning on vacations, or a down payment for another mortgage. When you look at the cumulative effect of paying this monthly and multiply it over five years, $30,000 of her hard-earned money goes towards interest. She is signing her paycheck over to a stranger.

I explained to her that even though the minimum balance is low for the month and she has some short-term financial flexibility, she is cheating herself over the long run.

To be a "thousandaire," you must first learn how to think small. Let us go back to the building a house analogy. If you decided to say I want to build a house, you must go through several administrative steps. After completing the administrative steps, such as pre-qualification and having the appropriate down payment money, you find a builder for your new house. There is no need to get into specifics as to whether or not you wish to build a custom home or select a floor plan for this example, as I want to create a simple picture in your mind. When you decided on how you wish your new home should look like, the ground is leveled or excavated, and the foundation of the house begins.

That foundation of your financial success begins with you. Although there are numerous quick fixes to additional streams of income or having so much credit, you should not take the easy path in creating the foundation of your financial fitness. Imagine during the construction of your new home; the project manager proposes a quicker fix to build your home about a month and a half faster, but you would have to sacrifice some of the most reliable materials for cheaper materials. You would more likely than not accept that as you would like the best for your home. If that is the case, adjust your thinking that your financial fitness is akin to building your home.

Worksheet #11 helps create the first steps of building your foundation. This book will not present sure-fire ways to become debt free. Although there are numerous of books discussing how to be financially secure in a year or how to lower your debt aggressively, the one common trait in all of those books is discipline. I hope this book will be the bridge for you to explore other books once you have the discipline, as there is some good material out there. However, the purpose of this book is to help you create a foundation of personal development in a manner that you can incorporate this into your daily life and routines without requiring you to place additional burdens and stress on yourself to achieve financial prosperity. Remember, the only person who can define your success is you.

In this exercise, you will identify the debt that you currently have and the interest that you are paying. We will exclude your mortgage and student loan debt if you happen to have these expenses, as they tend to be costs you will carry for many years under most assumptions. The debt you will identify that you are responsible for is something you would like to be conscious of rather than continuing to opening your statement and making the minimum payments.

After you complete this exercise, try sticking the worksheet somewhere where you can see it more than once. For every time you see how much money that you are giving away monthly, it should light a fire in you to try to get this paid off as quickly as possible. It is feasible to pay these bills off if you have a plan. This entire book and each worksheet help you identify your plan, and provides you with some essential tools to create a way to execute your plan.

Axiom #12: Being debt-free does not send you to jail

As I said several times throughout this book, I am writing this book from the perspective of most hard-working Americans who works a full-time job and relies on a regular paycheck to handle mandatory and discretionary expenses. Even though at this moment, I have enough set to the side to survive for over six months, I cannot afford to be on the sidelines long without any income.

In the past, we could define the breadwinner of the household as the individual who worked, and the other parent would stay at home and raise the kids. In this era, and for the unforeseeable future, you will need at least two incomes if you are married. If you are a single parent, you have to be creative and flexible with the income you bring in if you only have one job. I am quite certain that we can all agree that we must be creative in managing your income. As we continue to bring in our normal paychecks, we constantly get a stream of mail advertising credit cards, car buybacks, and mortgage refinancing. Almost every store you go to now has its own credit card with its own rewards program. As in most cases, we have often dipped into our credit card to pay for auto repairs, major purchases, or even entertainment expenses.

It is almost as if we are brainwashed to believe that credit is our only way of life. From the homes that we live in, the vehicles we drive, and often time, the clothes on our backs. Let us not talk about student loan debt, which the majority of us who have gone to school, including yours truly, have incurred relentlessly over the course of our college careers. All the while we continue to incur this mountain of debt, we continue to go about our everyday lives and making our minimal payments and continuing to do whatever it is that make us content and happy.

I am here to tell you that when you borrow, you owe. It sounds simple; however, it is an addiction plaguing millions of Americans, young and old. While we continue to pick up an extraordinary amount of debt, we continue to claim that this is ours. The cold reality is that it is not. The house you live in more than likely belongs to the bank. The car you have where you are currently making payments belongs to the bank. In the event you miss your payments for a consecutive stretch, the lending party has the right to retrieve the property from you. If you are borrowing heavily through credit cards, you are paying for items you charged up years ago if you are not making any realistic efforts to pay off your debt. Even though no one will knock on your door to take those items, you pay dearly in interest and fees.

Here is another way to look at the credit card dilemma. The average annual percentage rate is 14.9%. Your 401k may have a rate of return from 4-8% year over year. Now let us do the math. If you have a $7,500 balance on a credit card, you are accruing approximately $1,117.50 in interest fees. These fees go directly back to the bank, and not into your pockets. If you have a 401k with the same balance, you earn approximately $600 in dividends over the same course of time. These assumptions are on the premise you are not contributing towards your 401k for the year, and the balance of the credit card remains $7,500 throughout the entire year.

Now think about what you can do with the roughly $500 difference you are giving away. Imagine if you were able to charge yourself interest by paying an extra $1,117.50 towards your investments. When you talk to the average person, they are content on paying the minimal balance towards their debt, all the while not paying attention to interest paid to credit card companies and banks. I do understand that despite new consumer protection laws concerning credit card statements they are still intimidating to read. However, the simple nature of this axiom reminds you that you are capable of controlling your financial destiny if you are willing to make certain adjustments.

One thing you have to keep in mind is that despite what the experts in their field tell you, you are still responsible for knowledge of your own finances. Many "experts" exist to capitalize on your greed and your lack of fundamental understanding of how the markets work. As harsh as this may sound, it is true. For example, let us look at your car insurance. Most people do not realize that it is more expensive to pay your car insurance payments throughout the entire year instead of an annual payment. Monthly payments allow the insurance company to charge fees, as well as accrue interest on your payments, which is similar to paying your credit card bills. Although paying monthly is more convenient, you could possibly save up to 30% off your premium if you pay your insurance on an annual basis. For example, if you and your spouse owe $825 for the entire year, and you were able to capitalize off the 30% deduction for paying it off early, you will save approximately $247.50. To simplify this more, you could save over $20 a month in monthly payments.

Another example of the credit crunch exists within the mortgage industry. The financial sector has capitalized on the American dream of homeownership. Despite the creative ways for financing, the amount you pay on the remaining balance of your mortgage is exponentially higher than what you originally signed on the contracts. The amount owed for mortgages today creates more difficulties for those who are seeking to be debt-free without a plan. In 1970, 39% of homeowners did not have a mortgage versus 29.3% as of 2013[5]. This means that close to 70% of homeowners do not own their home free and clear.

To put this in more perspective, if you are averaging $3,500 per year in mortgage interest over a span of 30 years for a typical 30-year loan, you will pay $105,000 towards interest. This does not include any refinance or additional fees. Think about this fact for a minute. For years, you heard that it is best to invest in a retirement account (which is true), and your home is one of your greatest assets (which is true); however, you are spending a large percentage of your take-home pay towards lining the pockets of the banks who try to sell you that the American dream is best for you.

I am not diminishing the value of home ownership. As I stated before, I am currently in your situation in owing on a home. However, when you think about the money you could save by investing some of that into other areas, you are investing in yourself. The next axiom will go into more details about building and become your brand. For this axiom, the goal is to expand the scope of your consciousness and thinking of how can you attempt to eliminate debt.

Understanding how debt affects your financial health is a major component of the Financial Fit. When I talk to others about their debt situation, I often hear them speaking like it is the plague, but they are not willing to see their physician for any exclusive remedies. Despite the amount of debt incurred, some of the same people whom I have spoken to continue to swipe their cards to obtain things they could not necessarily afford. Unfortunately, there are those who may have extenuating circumstances such as children with special needs, high medical bills due to unexpected illnesses, or caring for a family member which may limit their ability to pay down debt. Despite these challenges becoming more conscious with your money and living within your means lowers additional stress associated with calls during the bill collection process.

---

5 http://www.doctorhousingbubble.com/americans-that-own-home-with-no-mortgage-free-and-clear/

By understanding how your money works effectively to you creates opportunities for you later on down the road. Unless you win the lottery or some other significant financial windfall, you will not have a ton of money in your accounts. Dedicating yourself to financial responsibility and understanding how your paychecks can work best for you grows your accounts in ways that create less of a reliance on credit cards. The best way to address your financial situation and identifying ways to grow financially is through budgeting.

Budgeting takes time, patience, and discipline. If you are still a compulsive shopper or spender in general, you will find that budgeting is very difficult. I always consider budgeting as similar to dieting. The goals and intentions of what you have in mind make sense; however, the lack of discipline and focus limits your ability to lose weight or save money. What I would like to point out about budgeting is that doing so does not make you a cheapskate or frugal. Budgeting is a way to identify and implement realistic goals. Similar to the Spiritual/Mental and Emotional Fits, being pragmatic and realistic can go a long way in your overall personal development.

When you start budgeting, you must be able to look yourself in the mirror figuratively. You should be comfortable and understanding of your financial health and your current situation. If you are in denial or attempting to avoid certain expenses to make your budget on paper look good, you deny yourself an opportunity to get a grasp of your situation. Take control of your financial situation by understanding that you may have made some poor financial decisions; however, you control your destiny. Controlling your destiny comes with the territory of managing your financial situation.

When creating your budget, you will need to set goals. Your first set of goals should be something that is quickly attainable. By making the first round of goals attainable, you will be able to see the small victories mount up quickly. What you do not want to do is set your goals that take a long time to accomplish. If you are not a homeowner and wish to put a reasonable down payment, the length of time to take you to save may affect the way that you are looking at your current budget. If you have a credit card that has $500-$1,000, use that card as your first goal to see the tangible results right away.

Flexibility makes a good budget. Even though it is doable, keeping the budget the same on December 1 as you had it set on March 1 is challenging. The reason why includes emergency bills, unexpected repairs to your vehicle, clothing you may have to purchase for a job interview, or even birthday/holiday celebrations. Do not be so fixated and obsessed with your budget that you begin to stress out about it. You will have some months where you may be in the red with more money spent than projected. This happens in real life, as well as the business world. One of your goals in setting your budget is to set it where you are in the black more often than in the red. Even if you wound up saving $20.53 at the end of the month from your budget, it is still better than spending $20.53 more than what was originally budgeted.

Budgets should not be restrictive to the point where it is unrealistic. As stated several times throughout the book, this is a personal motivation, a self-development book for your lifestyle. I encourage you to make sure that you continue to maintain a work-life balance. You should set some time and money to enjoy whatever it is you like; however, I encourage you to do so responsibly. Your budget should be reflective of your work-life balance and freedom of life that you so very much deserve. One of the keys when setting your budget is that you are living within your means. If you are cognizant of this, I believe that you will see small incremental gains and moral victories. In time, you will see your accounts grow, your debt lower, and your emergency funds continue to grow.

There is no worksheet associated with this axiom. As no two budgets will be the same, I encourage you to research some good budgeting tools and strategies to help set up your budget. You have different circumstances in life compared to others. Therefore, trying to provide you one budget template is not realistic for everyone. This axiom serves as a bridge to the last axiom under the Financial Fit. Remember being debt-free is a luxury, and it is not a crime. Although everyone's situation is relatively different, it is possible to eliminate debt and grow your financial worth over the course of time.

Axiom #13: You are your own brand. Learn how to invest in it.

We love to buy, wear, or use numerous brands. Outside of the name recognition, the products are often of reliable quality and comfort. With an increase of disposable income that is more abundant in these past two generations and other generations moving forward, personal consumption of products, goods, and services continue to increase. Think of the many options this current era provides that we did not have in years past from cable, internet, clothing stores, automobiles, and even lavish vacations. Regular routines we often take for granted today were a luxury in the past such as eating out, going to the movies or even viewing a sporting event.

As you recall under the Emotional Fit, I provided an axiom that noted how you should evolve your thinking from a want to would like. We find ourselves so preoccupied in wanting something that we disproportionately misjudge the value of importance and worth to our personal world. Because we overextend ourselves in our decision-making, we tend to make irrational decisions. Some of the decisions, particularly when it comes to some of our financial decision-making, puts us in a long term bind that we often find ourselves regretting years down the road.

Our purchases are often fueled by materialistic means. Some buy a particular brand of car, truck or SUV. Some are fixated on a particular purse or handbag. Some are fixated in their collection of shoes and name-brand clothing. Although that I am not against having some of the nicer things this world has to offer, what I do observe is there are many whose priorities are not in order. What I mean by not having their priorities are not in order is that I see others are willing to spend more towards an item or make monthly payments that rob them of what limited earning capacities they have.

I recall a conversation with a young woman who had a luxury car. I had an affordable mid-sized sedan that was highly rated for its performance and quality. One day, we happened to be walking to the same parking lot, and she had this puzzled look on her face as to what type of car I had. I told her, which was a 5-star rated sedan, and she replied that she was not aware of this particular model from the brand name. She then asked me why I did not have a luxury car and that is all she drives. Even though I did not feel like comparing financial situations, what I did know about her is that her luxury vehicle and her current situation of living in an older apartment did not fit the bill of her perceived status of this luxury car. Despite this mental note, I did inform her that if I wanted to have a luxury car, I could; however, I did not feel like handling the maintenance expenses associated with those vehicles knowing how much money I made at the time as well as how often I would be using that car. Two weeks later, she asked me for gas money and stated that she could pay me back when she when paid the following week. She never paid me back.

Although this is not a shot at this particular woman, in my mind, well before I began my personal journey of the Four Fits, I knew then that having a luxury vehicle at that time was not conducive to my current lifestyle and lifestyle choices. Her anticipated expenses for her car, which would include car, note, maintenance expenses, and including gas, are significantly higher than my expenses. I would imagine that the difference would be close to $250/month, which is a conservative estimate. Simple math shows that $250 in savings monthly equates to $3,000 a year in savings. Our salaries were likely identical; however, even if she made marginally more than me, the net loss would negate any potential for positive financial growth.

Before I continue to expand into this axiom; I do recommend *The Millionaire Next Door* by Dr. Thomas J. Stanley and Dr. William D. Danko, as well as the *Total Money Makeover* by Dave Ramsey for those who feel that they have the discipline and wherewithal to attack their debt and increase their financial net worth. Again, as the purpose of this book is to lay a foundation of sorts, I do not want to dive too deep into financial management, as you must understand the fundamental elements of your spending, investing, and purchasing behaviors first. Therefore, if you feel like you need to continue to expand upon this foundation, I encourage you to continue reading literature from those authors, among others and enhancing this axiom.

You are your brand. Your name is your legacy, for which you can leave your children, family, and friends something to build upon. The definition of wealth is "taking the total market value of all the physical and intangible assets of the entity and then subtracting all debts[6]." Whatever you plan to leave behind for your next of kin can continue to grow to pass down from generation to generation. Before the advent of stock markets and mutual funds, land was considered a valuable asset that was passed down from generation to generation. Often, you hear stories of how certain farmland or ranches are a third or fourth generation. This is due to their property being passed down to their next of kin.

When you are purchasing a particular brand name, you are unknowingly providing additional revenue for another person's legacy to be extended from generation to generation. Although spending money is inevitable, the key to this axiom presented to you is this question, "How much are you willing to purchase onto yourself?" Alternatively, another way to present this question is, "How much is your brand worth?"

The key premise of this axiom is not stating that you should start your clothing, food, or vehicle line. The premise of this axiom is for you to recognize the worth that you have invested towards yourself. Even though others are not necessarily running to the stores to purchase you, you are responsible for investing that money to continue to grow your overall value, your worth, and your brand. By developing your brand, you continue to present yourself opportunities that allow you to make solid decisions with your personal finances.

---

6 Definition of "Wealth" http://www.investopedia.com/terms/w/wealth.asp

Before diving deeper about understanding yourself as your brand, let us look into your level of understanding of finances. To move in an area where you are comfortable with your financial management, you must develop an understanding of general finances. Remember, your name is your brand. In the spirit of the Four Fits, you should continue your focus on personal development and lay the foundation for how you can grow. Your vision of being financially prosperous, if that is what you seek, cannot manifest unless you are willing to take the time to understand the general principles of finances. I will provide you another example to illustrate this point.

I know of a young woman who appeared to be doing well, based on her appearance of her and her family on social media. She continued to post photo after photo of her lavishes, with numerous statements of how she is making her money. I asked her one day when I saw her if she knew the difference between making money and earning money. I also asked if she knew anything about mutual funds.

To the first question, she replied that she was making money based on her job endeavors. She further stated that she did not know anything about mutual funds, but she was willing to learn. I explained to her that most 9-5 jobs or "W-2" jobs earn money. When you are earning money, you must report to work or provide some level of acceptable output or performances to remain employed and earn a check on the designated paydays. Thus, why you see questions whether they are tax forms or of the like, you will see what your current "earnings" are. When you are making money, you do not necessarily need to be physically present to have your income grow. You have different avenues to find ways to have your money grow and under most instances reinvest to continue to fund your financial interests.

The answer to the second question was that she did not know anything about mutual funds. To that, I am not surprised, but I asked her if she was interested in learning how to make money and to educate her about the distinction of those two. She stated that she was interested because she did not know what they were. She indicated that she was interested in some projections that I learned from reading other financial literature found on popular financial websites. I explained to her about my axiom about building herself as her brand. Despite setting a personal calendar reminder to find out what she learned and if she took any steps, she was dismissive of the idea. Yet, she continues to post many images of her lavishness.

It is unreasonable to expect that everyone will exercise restraint or a solid understanding of financial management. To many, it is a daunting and intimidating task. However, many do crave to live a life without crushing debt and not working past their 60's. Despite this desire, many do not have the discipline to learn the simple 123's of increasing their likelihood of achieving their long-term vision. As you may recall under the mental fit, you are tasked to develop and track your short, intermediate, and long-term plans by using measures of one, three, and five years. Your ability to be financially secure takes place by incorporating the 123's of financial understanding into your overall comprehensive plan.

A 2014 study conducted by the Federal Reserve System estimated that approximately 65% of private-sector workers had access to retirement plans through their jobs. Unfortunately, 48% participated in an employer-sponsored plan, with 40% not even participating in any retirement plans.[7] The numbers of private sector workers who underfund their employer-sponsored plans are also relatively high. This reinforces the fact that despite their wishes to retire at a reasonable age, many will face or are confronting the stark reality that they will not have enough money to retire.

Before completing the next exercise, I want to discuss time deposits, which includes checking and saving accounts. If you advance to the point where you have positive net worth and have a considerable amount of finances and assets available, you are essentially self-insured. You are capable of taking care of your financial needs despite changes under

---

7 "The Reality of the Retirement Crisis" Center for American Progress, https://www.americanprogress.org/issues/economy/report/2015/01/26/105394/the-reality-of-the-retirement-crisis/

most normal circumstances. A vast majority of us, including myself, are not at this level or reasonably close. Does that mean that we cannot achieve this level of security? We can reach this level; however, it takes discipline and perseverance.

Checking and savings account do not yield much interest in comparison with other investment options available. Also, the immediate accessibility to obtain cash may present a downside, as it is a common habit to withdraw money just to have money. Furthermore, fees exist under most checking and savings account, which is interesting because it is encouraged that you have these options, but you could incur fees that could be as punishing as having a credit card account. As you are trying to build yourself within the Financial Fit, you should understand that your checking and savings should be used as a short-term account. If you utilize reliable techniques for saving your finances by putting a small amount to the side in savings and using a budget, you will grow your account to the point where it resembles your personal line of credit. Although there are different arguments as to what is best for you, I believe that as you continue to build your brand, maintaining approximately $1,000 - $1,500 in checking and $1,500 - $2,000 in savings would provide you sufficient income to address your short-term needs. This includes minor vehicle expenses/repairs, clothing, and general miscellaneous needs.

Finding the small victories in your planning makes a difference in the end. It boosts your confidence, and you can see the tangible differences from where you are today, and where you were months ago. Even if you are putting $25 a month aside, you will have $250 at the end of the year. If you feel you are sandwiched with debt and feel like you cannot get ahead, think about all that you do throughout each month. Try to find where you can save $25. If you like to drink or smoke, which are expensive habits, you can easily save that by not smoking cigarettes for one week, or not buy any alcohol for the entire weekend.

Are you a chronic "order outter?" If you order out for lunch 4-5 times a week, you would be amazed how much you spend each week. The average

American spends approximately $53 a week on eating out for lunch[8]. That totals close to $215 a month, or close to $3,000 a year! Those figures do not even take account if you eat out for dinner often with a family or by yourself. If you took a fraction of that and not ordered for lunch, that $25 you can save in that month equates to $46.75 weekly under the same assumption. If you wanted to save $50 a month, you could do so by cutting down to $40.50 a week. So, if eating out is your vice (which we will discuss more under the Physical Fit), you can continue to eat out, but save money by cutting down once or twice each week.

Another example of how you can build your brand is something that you typically contribute to without thinking much about it, warranties. The money you invest in warranties could be invested into yourself. This statement holds true if you have been able to build a rainy day or emergency fund to cover costs of most general repairs. You may initially balk about considering in pocketing the money away that you would put towards warranties, but several reasons exist why this is a recommended practice.

Most warranties are offered in different industries as another tool to have you contribute more to their bottom line. Warranties offered to tend to play on your emotions as consumers and not necessarily the defective rate of the product itself. Most expensive equipment purchased will likely become defective within their original warranty period. The likelihood of that product becoming defective decreases over time until original wear and tear kicks in, which is inevitable. Most consumers do not research the failure rates of products. Some warranties offered are more than 20% of the original value of the purchased item, which analysts do not recommend purchasing. Ultimately, paying for the repair is cheaper than paying the extended warranty, which in some cases; carry on for months and months on end.

If you are in the process of building your brand, your brand should move in an effort to self-insure yourself. Removing yourself from the

---

8 "Survey: Eating lunch hits the wallet $53 a week on average, Southerners spend the most." http://talkbusiness.net/2015/11/survey-eating-lunch-hits-the-wallet-53-a-week-on-average-southerners-spend-the-most/

grasps of debt and use of credit cards will be difficult; however, you can slowly begin to create ways to become less reliant on the use of credit. Let us go back to equipment that is relatively expensive for a large purchase such as items for your house. The refrigerator, stove, or water heater costs hundreds of dollars. The warranty that is offered by most companies tends to run anywhere from $50-$75 a month. When you factor in service calls, you could pay $125 or more for something that could or could not be covered under warranty. If you put that $50 a month in your funds for emergency/repair fund, you would have $650. Over three years, you would have $1,850 put to the side, and this gains interest. Keep in mind that the alternative is you paying a company to hold your money, and gain interest on what you are giving them to hold.

Obviously, this rule may not apply to all situations, as older homes may cause concern for repairs, especially if you have depleted your funds after making a move. Having this put to the side will help you maintain financial growth and peace of mind. How often have you heard your friends say that their fridge went out, and they do not have the money for another one? Had the money been put to the side, most if not all the costs would be available to buy another one.

Before you begin to state you do not have the money, remember you are paying someone monthly, voluntarily, out of your pocket. For example, I spoke about this concept to someone about her phone warranty. Her rationale is that her phone is $600 for a replacement without the warranty. I informed her that paying $600 is $60 a month for ten months or $50 a month for 12 months. If she paid the warranty for 24 months at $10 a month, she would pay $240 for a $600 phone. However, if you are putting the money aside, knowing that you will always have a phone, you will have your warranty over time for your replacements, if needed. My counterpoint to this would be, if you have to buy new tires for $600, would you put $10 a month aside for warranty for your tires?

Those are several examples that you can use to understand how you can build your brand. The next worksheet will assist you in determining other ways you can build your brand from within. Identifying ways to cut your costs can go a long way in creating financial stability, and provide you opportunities to do some of the things you would like to do without being so dependent on credit. The goal of understanding how you build your brand is to know how to remove dependent behaviors. Credit card and credit dependency strip your ability to save, invest, or even spend your hard-earned dollars. Numerous stores offer you credit cards with buyback options to entice you to spend. Although cash back options are great, I would recommend using a rewards program where you are using your checking account so that you are not incurring interest. If you do use a credit card's cash back option, ensure that you are paying off your purchases before the next billing cycle.

When completing this exercise, be sure that you are honest with yourself. You want to develop a plan that is realistic and reasonable. You do not want to create a plan you are consciously aware that you do not have the discipline at this time. The most common mistake that people make about committing to making wholesale changes is that they aim at a level that is devoid of the fundamental understanding of how to get there in the first place. You cannot become the most valuable player of a sport unless you learn how to put in the dedication and hard work to get there in the first place.

The best advice that I can give you in completing this exercise is to keep it very simple. Become aware of the person you are from your spending habits to how serious you are about saving. By becoming realistic with yourself, you will learn some interesting things about yourself. You will learn more about your desire for enhancing your discipline, and in the process, you develop a deeper understanding of what motivates you in attaining where you would like to be and winning that battle over what you want.

CHAPTER 5

THE PHYSICAL FIT

THE FINAL FIT of the Four Fits is the Physical Fit. At this point, you have started the path towards your personal development by addressing three areas that affect the majority of us during the daily grind called life. The key to the entire process of the Four Fits is to remember that your life does not exist in a box. Living figuratively in a box means you cannot see past the four walls that surround your life. Learning how to see outside the box expands your consciousness, as well as well expanding your horizons.

The Physical Fit focuses on your physical health and the perils that could be present in your life. Recall the Spiritual/Mental and Emotional Fit and some of the familiar concepts from within these Fits. To develop the concepts of the Physical Fit, you must find the inner strength from within to remain disciplined and consistent in those beliefs. The Physical Fit relies on your ability to identify what works best for you, and not what is best for everyone else.

You live within the confines of your skin. You are the first person to see yourself whenever you look in the mirror. You are also responsible for the intake of food and nourishment in your body. You are responsible for how many hours your sleep, and how often you smile and laugh. Your physical being is the temple where everything flows. The other Fits are pieces to keeping you physically viable and vibrant. I will link the reasons why each Fit relates to the Physical Fit below.

The aspects of the Spiritual/Mental Fit provide a template for your physical being. Carrying stress can be detrimental to you in so many ways. This is also true regarding the Physical Fit. Stress creates a negative reaction within your body that causes distress. Distress could lead to upset stomach, headaches, elevated blood pressure, and chest pain among other physical factors. Stress also affects the ability for you to concentrate. Depending on your work or personal activities, this lack of focus may place you in dangerous situations as your ability to process information diminishes. Therefore, carrying a positive mental profile plays well in developing your Physical Fit.

Earlier in this book, we discussed the Emotional Fit and the concept of removing your emotions from making business decisions. Although the premise was to explore using virtually all your situations and interactions in a businesslike concept, the lack of your emotions could negatively affect you physically as well. Such swings of your emotions could lead to depression, stress, or substance abuse. Similar to your mental state, your emotions could elevate your blood pressure. If you develop a co-dependency of sorts, you are not paying attention as much as you would like to your body.

The interrelated nature of your mental and emotional health in relation to your physical can be positive if you are willing to keep it nurtured in a healthy fashion. Studies show that positive relationships between mental/emotional and your physical creates the ability for your body to get more rest, increase your metabolism, keeps your body more refreshed along with intangible benefits such as peace of mind and serenity. Keeping a positive profile, which is a theme throughout the Four Fits, is central to the belief that your total self-awareness will grow. This ongoing growth will produce positive results for your well-being.

The Financial Fit does have a relationship to the Physical Fit. If you are seeking to become more fit financially, you must have a certain level of discipline and consistency. The same applies to your physical fitness. If you are trying to lose weight, you cannot do so if you lack the discipline to eat the right foods or perform the appropriate amount of exercises. Your commitment to improving yourself financially and physically starts from within. You have to possess the will and desire to become fit in both areas. You may also be willing to make different choices in spending your money eating out or buying food that is healthier in nature. The choices that you make regarding your Physical Fit created by you should fit your lifestyle effectively.

The next three axioms of the Physical Fit focuses on the combination of one axiom to each of the three other fits. Doing so creates a connectivity that underscores the relationship of the entire Four Fits concept. The first axiom connects to your Spiritual/Mental fit. The second axiom connects to your Emotional and Physical Fits. The third axiom focuses on how your financial decisions and lifestyle choices affect your Physical Fit.

Assuming that many of us are not looking like America's Next Top Model at this moment, the focus of the Physical Fit is set to accomplish realistic means of accepting who you are. However, you are responsible for making the appropriate tweaks to your mode of thinking in bettering yourself. Millions of us annually make commitments to weight loss and wholesale physical changes. Despite the announced intentions, whether it is at New Year's or for a special event such as weddings and vacations, you unknowingly place psychological pressure into achieving those goals. Thus, the stress and pressure to meet these goals make the process more agonizing, particularly if you are not successful.

Therefore, the purpose of the Physical Fit is to create something reasonable and attainable as a process of your life's routine. Being able to reach certain achievable milestones that are actionable and attainable will produce minor victories that have more of a pleasing psychological effect. Even if you have to start each axiom and exercise over, you do not feel ashamed for not reaching your goals. Once you can create enough momentum in working towards attaining your goals, you will become more motivated to expand to more high energy, high impact physical fitness goals.

Axiom 14: Find the right diet that is right for you

As you may recall under the Spiritual/Mental fit, you had to come up with your 12 Months of Progress (Worksheet 3). The purpose of this exercise was to challenge you to become more disciplined in your approach to whatever goals you set for yourself. It is easy to speak out what you wish to accomplish. Your mental resolve to accomplish each goal you have set to achieve. Once you began to document your progress and monitor it at regular intervals, you likely were able to make each task easier to achieve because you developed the mental capacity and strength to accomplish it.

What you put into your body daily plays a long way into your physical being. The majority of Americans are overweight. According to the National Institute of Health, two out of three adults are overweight or obese[9]. This statement is not an indictment of your particular weight situation if this applies to you, this is statistic should illustrate that there are 67% of Americans who are in a similar situation when it comes to weight. Despite the images flooded in our TV sets, magazines, and social media, the majority of people whom we see in everyday life are not models. I can state with relative confidence that a larger percentage of those identified as obese have tried some form of weight loss, commitments to exercise, or a physical trainer. I can also state with relative certainty that the majority of those who had tried, reverted to gaining more weight than when they first tried to lose it.

What you should take note about the above paragraph is that weight loss is a struggle. Weight loss and making an ideal weight will likely be a challenge for the majority of us for the rest of our lives. However, the focus of this axiom is to not directly state that you have to commit to extraordinary diets, workout routines, and financial commitments to weight loss. The focus of this axiom is to understand the most fundamental basic of attempting any weight control remedies, which is your diet. Consuming the right diet for you is a mindset that is ideal for you and your body. The person next door will eat differently than you, and vice versa.

---

9 National Institute of Health – National Institute of Diabetes and Digestive and Kidney Diseases. http://www.niddk.nih.gov/health-information/health-statistics/Pages/overweight-obesity-statistics.aspx

I will let you in on a little secret of mine concerning this topic, which is simple. Everyone is different. We all have different tastes and preferences of foods. Culture, race, geographic locations, and other variables influence the way that we eat and consume food. As such, whatever one person's method has for dieting may not be the most ideal for you. This is something that you should keep in mind in addressing whatever challenges you face in controlling your diet.

This axiom does not discredit the scientific research of the positive benefits of dieting a particular way. If you suffer from certain health ailments, it is highly recommended that you stick to what your physician recommended. This concept of dieting is simple to whatever is best for your lifestyle, but what is healthy for you as well. Your ability to eat right with regularity has positive benefits to your overall health. Such benefits include maintaining or lowering your weight, reducing the potential of chronic health ailments, preventing chronic health ailments from progressing worse and create a healthy mental state.

Dieting and your body's physical ability to consume and process foods depend on several factors. Your age, height, weight, and lifestyle could affect the ability for you to process foods. Your family history when it comes to hereditary ailments could also cause pause for you and your eating habits. Your daily activity level or lack thereof could affect how your body processes food as well. Knowing about your family history and your lifestyle plays a large part in understanding your body.

Knowing what you are eating is one of the biggest steps towards your dieting. When I speak of dieting, I am not speaking in the context of attempting to lose weight. I am speaking in the context of what your regular intake of food consists on a consistent basis. As more is required of us during not only the week but the weekend as well, it is easy to slip into poor eating habits. Also, it appears that at every turn, there is somewhere to eat. From fast food restaurants, casual fare, bar and grill, there is no short supply of places to eat. It also does not make it much easier when you stepped out in the parking lot and bombarded with the aroma of cooked food coming from the facilities. The challenges and temptations are unlimited.

Despite the numerous temptations and options available, many of the choices available are not truly healthy for us. Yes, it does taste very good; however, keep in mind how it affects our overall health. A third of calories consumed by Americans come from restaurants according to research. Research further concludes that the more you eat out, the chances of obesity increases. What is interesting to note is that eating out for lunch adds the most caloric intake compared to eating a prepared meal from home[10]. Let us go back to the Financial Fit conversation about eating out for lunch at an average of $53/week. This likely equates to eating out every day. If you are consuming on average an extra 160 calories a day for lunch only, you are consuming an additional 800 calories a week for lunch. Not only does eating out hurt the pocketbook, but it could also be harmful to your body.

Meal portions are remarkably different from what you prepare at home and what you eat at a restaurant. The portions of food you typically bring to work from home are in a small container, and likely do not contain many calories. At a restaurant; however, the sizes of the portions are larger. As you see the presentation on your plate and your eyes are transfixed on the food; you are more than likely tempted to eat the entire plate. This behavior could be attributed to how many of us were raised not to throw any food away, or eating everything that is on your plate. The play on our morals in a sense guilt us to eat more than what we should be eating, which leads to us being full.

Fast foods are one of the biggest culprits of obesity and potential health issues stemming from eating out too much. Most fast foods contain more calories than nutrition. There are numerous side effects from eating fast food frequently over time. Your digestive and cardiovascular systems are affected by elevated levels of sugar found from carbs and

---

10 "Eating restaurants boosts risk of obesity, experts warn." Marni Jameson, *Orlando Sentinel.* http://articles.orlandosentinel.com/2011-07-04/health/os-restaurants-obesity-20110704_1_restaurant-foods-eating-obesity-experts

additives. Trans fat and sodium raises your blood pressure, cholesterol levels, and causes an enlarged heart muscle over time. Other areas negatively affected by too much fast food in your diet include your respiratory and central nervous systems.

Although this is not a referendum against fast food restaurants and restaurants in general, the purpose is to raise awareness that what we eat has more of an impact on our bodies than just the calorie intake. As with everything else we do in life, what we do in moderation and away from excess is more beneficial for our mind, body, and spirit. If you seek to avoid being obese or desire to lower your weight to get out of obesity, the challenge starts with your mental ability to avoid putting stress on your body and organs from the quality of your food selections.

Psychological benefits exist from a proper diet. Eating the right foods may influence your mood and contribute to the mental energy you exude whether it is positive or negative. Research shows that eating healthy and being well balanced in your dieting choices helps with your mental health. Eating regularly and healthy can reduce depression, frequency of bipolar episodes, attention deficit/hyperactivity disorders, and limit the frequency of having anxiety[11]. For example, take a cup of coffee and the sugars that you have in your favorite cup. Similar to smoking cigarettes daily, your body becomes dependent on the caffeine and the sugar. Even though you may feel fine throughout the day, you unknowingly place additional stress on your nervous system. This results in irritability and a higher probability for anxiety.

Other benefits mental benefits exist from eating healthy on a regular basis. By having a balanced diet, you receive additional mental energy, and your brain remains more sharp and focused. Let us circle back to some of the exercises related to the Spiritual/Mental Fit. If you lack the energy and focus on a regular basis from poor dieting and poor eating choices, you may become more frustrated or even feeling that you cannot make it through your routine during the day or night. Whether

---

11 " Psychological Benefits of Eating Healthy," Alla Butler and Demand Media http:// livewell.jillianmichaels.com/psychological-benefits-eating-healthy-5062.html

you know it or not, your self-esteem is additionally affected by your eating habits. If you are seeking to improve your physique or lose weight in general, you will have a higher self-esteem and values of self-worth knowing that you are accomplishing your goals.

You do not have to eat like a gerbil for the rest of your life to be in harmony for the Four Fits process. I enjoy eating out; however, I do so from time to time. Sometimes my busy schedule and activities find myself not being able to cook as often as I would like; however, the choices I make assist me in making sure that I stay consistent with my goals. While at a fast food burger place, I will try to order something that is low in calories and see if the fat and sodium levels are low. I am also wary of salads unless I can make my own. When you order a salad from a restaurant or fast food restaurant, you could risk eating more calories and ingesting more sodium, trans fat, and cholesterol as if you were eating an entrée.

Even if you do not consider yourself significantly overweight or obese, do not fool yourself into thinking that some of the low-calorie menu items are always good for you. Normally, when I speak to people who are interested in losing weight, I like to the point that out concerning low-calorie count meals, processed meals, and prepackaged meals. Those seeking to lose weight focus more on their calories than the items that are in the food. If you are one of the people in this category, please reread the previous paragraphs concerning what is in the food. Most meals are still loaded with sodium, which tends to be more than what a person should intake in a given day. The same goes with fat grams. Therefore, the saying you are what you eat is very much true.

Assuming that most if not all people have a smartphone who is reading this book, please look up and download some of the free apps where you can track your calorie count, steps, and progress. When inputting what you are eating, you should monitor your fat and sodium intake. The FDA recommends that you should intake no more than 2,300 milligrams of sodium, and no more than 53 – 80 milligrams of fat a day. The intake is adjusted based on certain health criteria; however, what you are putting into your body when eating out in one setting sometimes comes dangerously close to reaching your limits. Take a Big Mac for example. A Big Mac has 29 grams of fat and 970 milligrams of sodium. Salads can be high in everything as well. A California Shrimp Salad at Applebee's has 840 calories, 66 grams of fat, and 3,490 milligrams. Therefore, despite the taste you are acquiring, you are sacrificing your health if you make eating out a routine.

The next exercise encourages you to confront your vices. I say this as we all have our vices. Being from St. Louis, I love Chinese food, BBQ, pizza, and a good burger. Even though I still eat them from time to time, I measure the portions to make sure that I do not eat to get full. Our bodies are not meant to be bloated and stretched when eating. I am confident most of us understand the feeling, yet we keep giving into doing so, which is due to several psychological and physiological reasons. As stated before, I do not want to guilt you for what you are eating, but I would like to raise awareness of what you are putting into your body.

The Physical Fit requires discipline in this area. You cannot have discipline if you do not have recognition. You should be able to recognize what is and what is not good for you. How much food you should consume, and when to push away from the table are goals for this axiom. If you are confident enough where you feel that you have your diet and appetite mastered, by all means, you should increase your exercise and challenge your body to excel. As you will see in the third axiom for this fit, your health overall depends on the sacrifices that you are willing to make early, and not too late.

This exercise addresses your dieting and recognizing what foods are harmful overall for your body. You should be able to discover what is loaded in some of your favorite meals and determine what is high in sodium, carbohydrates, and fat. This exercise will also require you to research what foods you believe are healthy for you to see what is truly healthy for you or not. Do not cheat yourself, but find ways to be creative. Remember, do not guilt yourself for what you are eating. Moderation is truly the key. If you are being moderate as to what you are eating and maintaining a healthy balance, you will see positive results.

Axiom 15: Understand the stressors in your life

Stress comes in a variety of ways. Some of the stress is physical, and some of the stress you encounter can be mental. Stress is something that we all must face in life; however, each person has a different way of managing it. Some people are creative with their ways in managing their stress. Others struggle with managing their stress, and their stress is compounded by the ways stemming from one event adding additional stress to another event.

In life, we encounter numerous stressors. Sometimes these stressors come from the workplace. The project that may last for several months that consumes the majority of your workday is an example. For some, stress comes through relationships. Raising children and maintaining a family are examples of stressors. Sometimes our children create an undue amount of stress. From a child with special needs or to a child that is always misbehaving, the amount of stress could be overwhelming at times. At times, stress comes from our regular routines in life from grocery shopping, commuting to and from work.

Stress affects men and women differently. Your personality type and physical makeup may also dictate how you manage stress. Stress may also negatively affect your mental health, which could lead to depression and substance abuse. Failure to recognize the stressors in your life may contribute or accelerate both. The way you decompress from a day full of stress affects the way your mind and body mends positively.

This axiom addresses stress and how it affects you by explaining the relationship with the Emotional Fit. In Worksheet #9, we discussed identifying the stressors in your life. In this axiom and the related exercises, you are to determine what stressors exist in your life, and how to create a balance between sanity and proverbial insanity. This axiom will also help you understand how stress affects you physically and emotionally. Being able to identify and combat the stressors in the routines mentioned above will help you become more balanced during your quest for holistic growth of the Four Fits.

Stress can be toxic for your health. The amount of stress that you put on your body happens over time so that one or two-time occurrence you have hit you later than at that moment. Most people when they complain about their stress levels, it is due to the cumulative effect of multiple stressors that become overwhelming to that individual. This creates physiological and psychological impacts towards the individual. Some ways that stress could affect you physically include poor diet, rapid heartbeat, loss of sleep, and an increase in your blood pressure. Other common side effects of stress include muscle tension, chest pain, headaches, and stomach pain.

Stress affects genders differently. Stress in women is handled and managed compared to men. Most men have fight or flight responses, where women tend to be more emotional and reasoning in their responses. When stress becomes consistent and chronic, it may become debilitating for women as the mental and physical toll becomes more difficult. Hormones play a role as to why there are gender differences between men and women, which leads to physical problems. Stress in men creates high blood pressure, change in sexual appetite, higher risks of heart attack, and potential for type 2 diabetes.

Despite these physical effects of stress, there are mental health issues that arise from excessive stress. Anxiety and restlessness may occur when you are under duress. You may find yourself more irritable or angry quicker. Concentration and focus diminish over time as stress continues to mount. The toll from stress may cause you to eat less and succumb yourself to some form of substance abuse. Unfortunately, with stress comes denial. You may be aware that you are stressed, but you tend not to realize how much stress you are under until it is too late. At this stage, some people may succumb to depression or prolonged state of sadness.

Your mental health and your emotional state are a balancing board for your lifestyle. Similar to wearing a pair of clothes that uplifts your mood when you are about to go out for a night on the town, positive mental health and emotions tend to lead to having you view life in a different outlook. You may find yourself more upbeat and more laid back to some matters that could stress other people out if they are under too much duress. Your mental health, if not taken care of appropriately, begins a downward spiral that is difficult for many to recover.

Your mental and emotional health affect your physical health. If these two are in jeopardy, your body begins to break down. This tends to be more prevalent when your stress moves from acute to chronic. Most anxiety and depression disorders come from chronic illnesses. No matter how strong you think you are, or how mentally resilient you may feel you are, the overwhelming nature of stress can be overwhelming. I can relate to this because this happened to me years ago.

I struggled with alcoholism and depression several years ago. I was never clinically diagnosed, but I suffered many of the telltale signs. I do enjoy drinking socially; however, during that period, I found myself drinking heavily. I went from drinking a couple of times a week to drinking every day. Often, I found myself vomiting in the morning because I was not eating much, but kept drinking heavily. When I got home from wherever, the moment I walked in the door to lay down, I would pass out and had difficulty remember what I said or done the night before. I became angry more often and displayed aggressive tendencies towards everyone. I often made poor decisions through my actions and from the words of my mouth. I hurt some good people and good friends with the sharpness of the words that came out of my mouth. Some of those relationships have yet to be fully restored.

My bouts with depression were not pretty as well. For many times, I would shut myself out from the world. I could accomplish routine functions such as going to work and take care of whatever responsibilities for that day, but my mind was not into it. I would go three or four days at almost regular intervals despondent and sit in a dark room, sometimes near tears. Sometimes the depression led to more excessive drinking and vice versa. I had issues for years that were deep rooted. Many nights, whenever I was able to sleep, my dreams were nightmares.

Certain triggers existed internally and externally that created the intensity of my stress. I did not manage my stress well. As a result, I quickly put on weight and was the heaviest at any other point in my life. Even though I was not a fitness buff, I did stay in the gym often, but during this turbulent period of my life that lasted for several years, I did not work out as much. I did not take care of my body as much, and it showed physically. Internally, my blood pressure continued to rise to the point where my medication had to change. I had increased gastric issues from a combination of drinking and stress, which resulted in extreme heartburn and other gastro-related problems. Many times, I felt that I was not going to make it to 40, more or less make it the next day. I had honestly lost my life's compass.

Some of you who are reading this can relate and have likely been through more. I do not wish to go into too many details, as it could be a book by itself; however, the point I am trying to make is that there is a light at the end of the tunnel if you are willing to believe one exists. The resulting stress from turning to alcohol or other forms of substance abuse plays havoc on your body. If you find yourself as a person going through this currently, you have to ask yourself is it worth it. The ongoing damage you are placing on your body over time sometimes cannot be repaired or reversed. Is it worth going through the scars of depression and substance abuse? For those who are near the end of life, some of our choices brought upon this particular stage of life. As stated before, stress that accumulates over time can be deadly. You have to ask yourself if you could picture yourself years down the road and imagine how your body will betray yourself years down the road, are you willing to make the adjustments now?

Relationships are another common form of stress. In a relationship, you are in a situation where parts of your identity may have to adjust or adapt to another person's personality to make the relationship work. For those who are in a relationship, the common goal that most are trying to achieve is a symbiotic relationship amongst the two people to co-exist in harmony. The synergy you share in a relationship can be very empowering. Unfortunately, in most situations, that synergy can be harmful and could leave long-lasting mental scars that may also affect your body.

Most relationships will not be a 50-50 partnership. You and your mate will bring different qualities to the table that makes your relationship unique compared to other relationships. When people begin making their relationship a unified effort, there will be friction. Conflict in relationships is inevitable. The level of conflict that occurs in relationships may become toxic if you allow it to be. If you are in an increasingly toxic relationship, you should begin looking for ways to exit the situation. If you find yourself to be in an abusive relationship, which includes mental and financial abuse, exiting should be considered an option. Some situations are easier than others to exit; however, your health and your general well-being should not be dictated by another person's will or problems.

Unlike dating in high school, relationships take as much effort as your regular workday. You may recall in a previous exercise where we discussed your love resume. To somewhat reverse the worksheet, imagine that your job has placed undue stress or untenable hours at work. What will you do? In some circumstances, you will begin looking for another job. You will decide that the situation is so unbearable with a bunch of strangers, that you are ready to leave. You claim that the job is stressful and you are willing to go. Unfortunately, we do not pull the same trigger when it comes to our relationships.

There are numerous reasons why stress exists in relationships. Some of the reasons include money, children, work-related stress, communication, and external factors. As stated before, life will continuously throw stressors in your life. Your ability to manage the stressors that come in your life lies within yourself. The toll of stress from relationships may negatively affect your sexuality, self-esteem, motivation, and self-awareness. For some, the stress caused by relationships creates high blood pressure, depression, substance abuse, eating and sleeping disorders. If you are seeking a relationship, similar to other stressors, you must be aware of what your stressors are in these situations.

Relationships are interesting, as it can be an exercise in futility. An average person may go through 10-15 relationships in a lifetime. These relationships do not necessarily have to be intimate or sexual. For all those relationships, you will find one (some more than one) who fits your ideal as "the one." That means that in your lifetime, you will have less than a 10% chance of your mate being the right one. If you put that in the context of a weather forecast, if you had a 10% chance of severe storms for a particular day, there is a high chance that it will be either clear or cloudy throughout the day than severe storms.

When you think of a failure rate like that, why are you investing so heavily and losing your mind for a relationship that is likely to fail? For those who are going out his or her way for their mate, take the time to love yourself and heal yourself before seriously engaging the next relationship. Otherwise, your failure rate goes higher. The damage you allow to yourself increases, and your stress level increases.

Workplace stress is the most common form of stress of virtually everyone who holds a job. Workplace stress is very common because you are constantly subjected to a set of stressors on a regular basis. For example, in a given work day, you are subjected to the stressors of time constraints, interpersonal relationships, unpredictability, and decision-making. Obviously, there are other examples of stress, but I believe these are the more identifiable. Now, I want you to think about or jot down the first five stressors that you encountered through work for an entire week. The majority of us may not even make it through Monday evening or Tuesday's lunch break.

If you truly did jot down all the stressors you encounter throughout a week; you will see that you are constantly subjected to a relentless barrage of stress. Even if you do not react to some stressors, they do take their toll. Even if you describe yourself as a laid-back individual who does not let much get under your skin, work does get under your skin. Maybe it is not as demonstrative as it is with others. Negativity, disgruntled employees, turnover, being short-staffed all adds a toll on you.

For some, the very nature of your position may create stress. A loss of powerlessness at work often exists due to the specific nature of your job, coupled with the fact that you are not permitted to express yourself in ways you could do outside the workplace. For some people, particularly for some based on their personality matrix, this creates additional anxiety and unease, which places a psychological toll on you. Due to some of our living situations and the obligations that we have towards family, children, or housing preferences, we place additional stress to and from work based on our commutes.

Learning how to cope with stress in the workplace is important as you spend a vast majority of your week going to work, either working or going home from work. Some of your worse habits regarding eating, lack of appropriate exercise, and exposures to stress come from the workplace. Even though you cannot eliminate stress completely from work, you can address the stressors by becoming active in diffusing stress. By diffusing stress, you are capable of releasing the tension from your mind and body.

Several strategies could assist you in lowering your stress. Time management and task management may help reduce your job stress. Some ways of addressing your time management are to create a balanced schedule, taking regular breaks, do not over commit your schedule, and make sure that you are jotting down reminders versus trying to remember everything you have to do in your mind. Some ways of addressing task management include prioritizing your duties, taking breaks between projects, be willing to compromise and not try to be the lead dog all the time and use available resources and tools to keep your tasks in line.

Creating a work-life balance is a balancing act that most people do not understand how to achieve this. A work-life balance exists when you can do what is necessary to you for work, and at the same time, keep a happy medium at home or away from the office. Work-life balance is the ability to separate home from work, and not allowing the stressors from work to permeate in your home life.

Learning how to create a bridge between work and life is the key to developing your work-life balance if you are struggling to create one. As stated before, we have the responsibilities of what we have at home or away from work, but what you do not want to do is to carry the stress with work throughout the evening as you try to tend to your life's obligations and responsibilities. Combining the two events will add even more stress into your life, which creates a toll on your body.

Being able to build in some "me" time is beneficial as you attempt to build the bridge between work and after-hours responsibilities. For example, even though the times I can do so differs because of the unpredictable nature and travels of my job (two stressors), I do allow time for myself to try to decompress. I try to mix up the activities that I do to decompress so that it does not feel routine to me. I enjoy video games, reading, watching the news, exercising, cooking, taking a nap, or just listening to music. Every morning when I wake up, I try to note what important matters I need to address when I get off work. I try to determine what would be a major or moral victory when I am free.

This process of thinking what I am going to do after work gives me something to look forward to doing. When I travel, I tend to have an idea of what I would like to do and commit to accomplishing that goal as soon as possible. If I tell myself that I am going to work out, I make that a priority because I am making myself a priority. You will not hear me talk too much about what I am going to do once I get to work or put too much energy into it because I know that work is stressful. I do not want to rob myself of the ability to enjoy my time before going to work. Typically, when I wake up, I give myself 45-60 minutes to do whatever I feel like doing in the process of getting ready to work so I do not feel rushed. I do so because I know that the majority of my day involves high-end decision making and thinking that drains me from time to time. Building in some "me time" gives me the opportunity to be free early in the day, give myself something to look forward at the end of the day or night, and allows me to spend enough time to deal with whatever tasks I have to address when I am home or any after-hours activity. This process takes away the stress or dread you may feel when you are about run errands.

You must take time for yourself as often as possible. Even if it is just 30-60 minutes in a day, doing so helps "reset" what you have in your day. We do have vigorous demands at work and home. However, we should not be so consumed and obsessed by it, that we feel the only time you able to have down time is on weekends or vacation. If that is the case, you will burn out and likely not enjoy the weekends and vacation because you put too much emphasis in your time off that you make trying to make your time off perfect, stressful.

Refer to the Emotional Fit and the exercises related to this Fit. Worksheets 8 through 10 helped you consciously recognize your emotions, and how to manage your emotions. Understanding your emotions and gaining control to create balance within yourself is important to address the everyday stressors you encounter. As stated earlier in this axiom, you are subjected to the relationship, workplace, and general life stressors necessarily every day. If you are not able to manage them, the stress will consume you and your body will deteriorate. Meditation, exercise, proper diet, and ensuring that you have adequate rest plays a long way in ensuring that your body has the mental, emotional, and physical ability to withstand the stressors you experience daily.

The next three exercises for the worksheet associated with this axiom focuses on the three areas discussed under this axiom. The first exercise covers your ability to recognize the stressors in your three common situations: general life, relationships, and in the workplace. Your goal is to briefly identify four stressors in each category and describe how it affects you physically. The purpose of this particular exercise is to bring awareness to what these stressors do to you, and how your body responds to that stress.

The second exercise for this worksheet helps you recognize your work-life balance. You should seek to understand where your bridge in your work-life balance is. On the left side of your bridge is your work. On the right side is your life. The hyphen in the word is you creating your balance. How do you seek or desire to build your bridge? How are you able to decompress from one gear to shift to another? Do you find yourself rapidly accelerating to the next set of events or stressors in your life to create additional friction? Remember, if you are not able to build a bridge for yourself, the ongoing stress that carries from one side to another will create instability and amplifies the next set of stressors you will encounter.

The third exercise for this exercise is identifying what strategies you can use to decompress yourself. Do not write something down that you realistically feel will be difficult to complete. You do not wish to add additional stress in trying to accomplish something that you may not have the time or energy to complete. At the same time, you do want to write something that is challenging, as well as something that you can chart along the way. Something as simple as reading a book or article to take your mind away, or take a quick walk in the neighborhood could suffice. One day I was chatting with a co-worker who was discussing that she wanted to work out but was hardly motivated to go to the gym. I recalled a conversation that she liked watching certain shows on the DVR. I encouraged her to consider using a mini-stepper or a basic elliptical to combine what she loves to do when she gets home as well as meeting her goal of working out without leaving the house. It may sound easier said than done for most, but again, if you set the timeout and understand that you are doing your body a favor, you may stop believing that working out is a chore in itself.

Ultimately, you are responsible for the input and output of what comes and out of your life. Stress is something you cannot honestly avoid; however; you can manage it if you attempt to have the right strategies to cope and disperse stress. Identifying stressors in your life, and how it negatively affects your physical and mental health, goes a long way in prolonging your life, as well as your relationship with others.

AXIOM 16: YOUR HEALTH DEPENDS ON YOU, WHAT WILL YOU DO ABOUT IT

Here is a flashing newsbreak: You only live once. Even though that statement is nothing new, we live a life as if we are guaranteed that we will have a second chance to make up all the missteps of the would have, could have, and should have all over again. The cold reality of life is that when it is over, it is over. So many times, we talk about someone we know that made some questionable lifestyle choices that ultimately led to their demise.

We only have once chance to make it right. I saved this axiom for last for several reasons. First, every axiom under the Four Fits helps provide a framework that you can follow your path towards personal development. What is unfortunate is that we expend so much effort and energy trying to have what we desire so much, we often forget to take care of the most important person in the world, you. Second, I have spoken at length about creating your definition of success. Although this is critical in understanding what is best for you, the question is how you can enjoy what you achieved if your body is failing you? Third, among the other axioms of the Physical Fit, this axiom ties into the entire concept of dieting and understanding the stressors of your life. The prior two axioms are interrelated to this one. Therefore, if you are in the practice of learning what it takes to accomplish the first two axioms, the concepts as outlined in this axiom will make more sense.

Unfortunately, as we place more physical and mental demands on us, we often ignore the warning signs that our body sends to us. Sometimes we spend more time trying to figure out what to wear, type of make-up to put on, the cologne or perfume for the desired fragrance, but often ignore the image that we see in front of the mirror. We often try to mask our deficiencies, and sometimes we wind up lying to ourselves about who we are or how we are truly feeling.

Previously, we looked at the effects of stress, as well as, what we put into our body regarding our diet. I would like for you to recall some of the exercises that you completed for the previous two axioms. For most of us filling out these sheets, you will probably realize how much stress we are putting on our mind and body. Internally, no one can continue to handle stress over a sustained period. As we continue to go through this axiom, I hope you can understand that you are not a machine. You have many responsibilities, so does everyone else. Each responsibility is different from another, but if you are not capable of staying fit mentally and emotionally, your body will fall apart physically. There is a distinct difference between chronic and acute. For the next discussion, we will cover these differences for stress and illnesses.

You are looking for your car keys, and running late. You have a presentation in front of several prospective clients, which could result in a new agreement for the company, as well as a raise for yourself. You are frantically looking everywhere for your keys. You found your keys underneath the mail, and you frantically run to the car trying to get to the meeting on time. Once you get to the meeting, you still feel your heart racing, and your mouth is dry.

The experience mentioned above is an example of acute stress. Acute stress comes from a precise or exact event where your body reacts in a stressful response. Acute stress comes from a variety of ways from a car cutting in front of you in traffic, a loud sound that makes you jump in your seat, or exposure to extreme temperatures. Acute stress can be avoidable or unavoidable depending on the extent of the event or occurrence. Regarding the lost car keys situation, placing your keys in the same spot every day minimizes the chances of you experiencing stress in the mornings. An argument with a friend or your significant other can be an example of acute stress if it is a specific situation and not an argument that extends over time.

Acute stress is short-lived and does not necessarily have to be negative. Cramming for a big exam for school or certification exams may cause acute stress to the point where you become more mentally sharp and aware. This stress is due to the adrenaline created by the anticipation of taking the exams, as well as recognizing the finality of the exams. Once you can complete the exams and do well, you feel a sense of relief and accomplishment. Other examples of acute stress could come from a car accident, a brief slip without a fall, or receiving your employee evaluation.

Sometimes acute stress can be very traumatic and harmful to your mental health. Post-traumatic stress disorder (PTSD) occurs from an acute stress event that creates a significant psychological shock. Although, most people recently think of PTSD from war, PTSD can come from other sources as well. If you witnessed a murder or the death of individual on the interstate, it could be the cause of PTSD. Victims displaced by Hurricane Katrina suffered from a variety of symptoms of PTSD due to flooding, looting, and violence near the Convention Center and Superdome. Symptoms of PTSD occur within days or weeks of the traumatic event as it negatively affects your mind, sleep, eating, and creates emotional detachment. If you do experience symptoms of PTSD or believe to have symptoms, please seek help from a mental health professional.

Chronic stress is the prolonged period of stressful related events or circumstances that occur throughout an indefinite period. Unlike a near car accident where you find your heart beating rapidly for a couple of minutes, chronic stress is rooted in deeper causes. Chronic stress is harmful to your body as the stressors, or the cumulative effect of stress provides more harm to your body, as it is repetitive. Sometimes chronic stress is similar to the movie Groundhog Day, where every day is the same. Sometimes, you may feel like your struggles are ongoing with no end in sight.

Earlier, I discussed acute stress symptoms and how fight or flight symptoms may occur. Imagine if someone's car alarm went off while you were in the house relaxing. This is an example of acute stress because your adrenaline is pumping due to being startled. Now, imagine if that same car alarm was going off for over an hour because the driver was unaware. The continued noise over time will grind on your nerves, and you become more frustrated. Over time, your heightened senses from the acute stress prolong. After the situation has been resolved, or you have removed yourself from the ongoing alarm, you may feel mentally and physically fatigued. This is a byproduct of chronic stress.

Imagine that you are a parent of a child who has special needs. Not every day is remotely the same as the day before. Often, you may not have two similar days in the same month. The sequence of events in raising a child with special needs, regardless of your family or financial dynamics, is stressful. The prolonged effects of stress create high levels of anxiety and irritability. Prolonged stress makes some relationships with others difficult, as certain words and events may be perceived in a different manner because you are under a level of duress that others may not experience. Parenting and raising children with challenges, whether it is medically diagnosed or behavioral, are examples of chronic stress events.

Increased exposure to chronic stress may create anxiety, depression, heart disease, sleep problems, and weight gain. In the previous axiom, we looked at identifying the stressors that exist within your reality. Identifying and removing those stressors, particularly the chronic stressors, are critical for keeping your physical and mental health at a healthy level. Once you are aware of what events or situations are creating chronic stress, you should develop effective methods for managing how this stress permeates in your everyday life.

Stress management is very effective regardless of where you are in life. As stated before, everyone experiences stress in some shape and fashion. For most people, they are subjected to stressful events on a daily basis. Your ability to manage stress depends on your ability to break down the stressor occurring and dispersing that negative energy. Creating a holistic mindset comes with the ability not to allow the stressors in your life dictate and control who you are. You cannot avoid all the stressors in your life, so it is critical for you to determine how you can manage your stress on a consistent basis.

Good stress management techniques produce positive effects on your physical and mental states. The less stress you carry within your psyche, the stronger your immune system becomes. You can sleep better, develop a more relaxed mood, have more energy throughout the day, and maintain a more positive attitude. Combating stress and the negative symptoms associated with it takes a toll on you. Please continue to refer to the exercises related to the previous axiom to assist you in managing your stress.

Illnesses are acute and chronic as well. Some illnesses may go away within a couple of hours or days, which is acute. However, some of the illnesses or conditions people experience may last for months, years, or an entire lifetime. These are chronic illnesses. Without specifically rehashing the differences between the two, one thing to keep in mind is that your acute illnesses may develop to chronic illnesses. If you have acute symptoms, do not hesitate to seek medical attention to treat them if the symptoms continue. Being proactive with lingering acute systems could prevent the development to a chronic illness.

Some of the chronic illnesses are genetic or hereditary. Despite this fact, you have the responsibility to make sure that you are addressing the issues head on without delay. Remember, you only live once. The more you neglect the warning signs or fail to keep your conditions in check, it becomes harder to reverse. For example, if you are a person who has hypertension that is hereditary, you cannot keep eating products high in sodium, skip your blood pressure medication, and expect your blood pressure to remain low, or go down. This is similar to you exercising at the gym and then eating a large bucket of popcorn loaded with butter and salt.

We all have our vices. Unless a physician tells you to avoid certain foods, activities, or beverages absolutely, you should be free to enjoy what you seek to enjoy, as long as it is in moderation. I know of someone who has high blood pressure and diabetes. He eats out fast food and carryout restaurant meals loaded with fat, sodium, and sugar. Even though he knows that this is not healthy for him, he continues to eat these foods. Unfortunately, as his health continues to deteriorate, some of the chronic symptoms could have been avoided by partaking more in moderation than with a high level of frequency.

Recall the axiom of this Fit concerning having the appropriate diet in your life. I remember when I used to drink heavily; I would also not eat right. When I tried working out, I felt ok, but I had a hard time losing weight or appearing fit. I started to become more bloated around the stomach. I was in denial because I did not understand how I could do that much working out, but struggled to try to slim down or lose weight. In fact, I was gaining weight during that stretch.

When people talk about losing weight, it is interesting to hear about the internal struggles they are having or the rationale as to why they are having issues losing weight. One of the key reasons why people struggle with losing weight is their away from the fitness routine discipline. A combination of appropriate diet and exercise will accelerate the weight loss process. However, people struggle with their individual discipline, which results in their struggle for their goals of losing weight. Your body will be whatever you elect to put into it. This includes working out and your proper diet.

Maintaining a positive relationship with your physician makes a difference as to how your overall health will be. If you have a positive relationship with your doctor, you tend to be more open with your lifestyle, symptoms, and other issues affecting your life. Even though the doctor is not right 100% of the time, their experience, research, and understanding of medicine provides better opportunities to make recommendations best for you and your current lifestyle. If you are not honest to your physician about your way of life or symptoms, the doctor cannot truly assist you. This is similar to the diet and exercise example I provided above. If you are not honest with yourself under both circumstances, you are not cheating anyone other than yourself.

Even though I am not a huge fan of prescription medicine or medicine in general, I have a healthy relationship with my physician who informs me what is best for my lifestyle. When I was in my 20's, I had a host of health ailments, some of it hereditary. Because of lifestyle choices I made, among other factors, I made my chronic conditions worse. If I had continued not to address my health issues, I would have been gambling with my life. I had too much to live for to risk throwing it away because I kept doing what I wanted to do. As you heard me say under the Emotional Fit, find a way to change your wants to would like. At that time, my desire to keep doing what I wanted to subject me to poorer health outcomes.

The last worksheet of this book is simple in nature. The exercise involved is nothing more than a checklist you should use to see where you are in managing your chronic and acute situations. This exercise also is a continuation of the previous axiom by identifying the stressors you have in your life. If you find yourself having symptoms where you may need to seek therapy or medical attention, please do not hesitate to do so. Seeking a mental health professional is nothing to be embarrassed. If you look for ways to make home improvements, you should also be willing to discover ways to improve your overall mental well-being.

This axiom, as well as the entire book, is by no means a substitute for issues that are chronic and require professional assistance. This book provides a foundation for you to build at your convenience. By asking to look internally and being honest about how you are feeling, and finding ways to address your concerns, you take the first crucial steps to enhance your life in a way that you find it fulfilling and holistic. Learning how to look inwards and recognizing your challenges are huge steps. Some people have challenges where most of them are self-inflicted. I understand this position because I used to be an expert of inflicting my challenges and adversity in my life. Over time, I was able to overcome them by changing my mindset and attitude, as well as developing a holistic mentality.

The purpose of this axiom is not to lecture you or to make you feel bad about what you are doing. Your desire to love yourself at your best relies on your ability to do whatever it takes to take care of yourself, physically and mentally. Understanding your health starts with you. Being in tune with your body and mind requires much work and a passion for achieving a healthy well-being. When I put this axiom together initially, I was thinking about how I like to sit outside and take in all the sights and sounds. I enjoy many aspects of life, and I seek and desire to find a way to put myself in a situation where I can continue to do so. Although some situations in life may prevent us from doing so long-term, most of us are capable of living our lives out in a manner where we have control of our destiny. Make the most of your situation, and take care of yourself.

Conclusion

THE FOUR FITS of Holistic Growth focuses on your ability to personally develop and grow within in four key areas: spiritual/mental, emotional, physical, and financial. The purpose of this book is to provide you a guide and a foundation for your growth. You are encouraged to take the path that is best for you. Feel free to apply whatever axioms you may believe that fits best under each of the fits.

When discussing the concept of this book with a friend of mine, we discussed parts of the Financial Fit. She mentioned couponing and the savings that come from along with purchasing store bought brands. I explained to her that the overarching goal of this book is to try to provide a compass for whatever works best for anyone who decides to embrace the core concepts of the book. Where she and numerous others may be stronger at the time and energy, it takes for couponing; others may struggle. Where some people could argue they do not have time to set for themselves, the same argument could be made concerning couponing.

The Four Fits of Holistic Growth is a simple book. When I started writing the material for this philosophy, I wanted to get away from sounding academic. I would like the book to appeal to anyone regardless of age, race, culture, or financial standing. A mistake from my perspective is that a book of this nature assumes that everyone is capable of doing whatever recommended from his or her vantage point. What I seek to achieve is that I provide you a broad, yet a simple look into how you can get over the hump in certain areas in your life by focusing you in a comprehensive, yet simplistic matter. Discipline and being able to embrace the realities of your situation are key determinants as to whether or not you can achieve the goals of the Four Fits.

The Four Fits works well if you can picture your life's four key areas in a circle or a sphere. Most diagrams commonly seen in print are designed in a triangle or a matrix designed box. The reason why I elected to use a sphere to design the Four Fits is to show the possibilities of achieving your success is infinite. The concept of the Four Fits takes that adage, "You can be whatever you set your heart or mind out to be," and adds context and structure to it. If you would like to have another visual, take a piece of paper and pen. Take that pin and start drawing in a circle, and keep extending the circle until you reach the end of the sheet of paper. The circle should resemble a fingerprint-like picture when you complete it.

When you make a comparison of what you drew on the piece of paper and the template you put it on, you will notice a distinct difference. The difference is that the paper that you used to draw the spiraling circle could continue to grow, but the piece of paper restricts that ongoing growth. The sheet of paper represents a boundary where once filled; you will have to get another piece of paper to add. In an ideal situation, you could continue to keep drawing the circle, which is why the Four Fits is as a philosophy of endless opportunities.

The Spiritual/Mental Fit was designed to lay the original foundation for the Four Fits. If you were able to build the discipline and mental resiliency needed to work on each axiom, the rest of the Fits would essentially fall in line. The first step in developing the Spiritual/Mental Fit was to understand who you are as a person, and where you have been during your journey in life. As we continue to inundate ourselves with responsibilities, we tend to forget all that we have accomplished to date. Sometimes, we find ourselves speaking on what we seek to achieve, but do not develop a plan that aims to accomplish our goals. Therefore, the Spiritual/Mental fit provides you a means to chart your progress; short, intermediate, and long-term plans; and learning how to turn your dreams into a vision, and vision to reality.

The Emotional Fit was the most interesting of all the Fits to discuss. Some people are more emotional and more emphatic than others. The challenge of this Fit was relatively straightforward in its constructs. For those who are more emotional than others, you will understand how your emotions could interfere with your ability to learn, listen, and, communicate. For those who may not be as emotional, understanding that having emotions is not a crime, but the challenge is learning how to tap into your emotions to connect with your potential. Finally, understanding the differences between wants and would like creates a balance of determining what is best for you as you continue to develop your growth.

I provided the Financial Fit third in the book as you ideally would be working towards your discipline and mental strength as the primary foundation for your growth. The Financial Fit helps define ways that you look at yourself as a brand. My brand is Dr. Terrence Duncan. Whatever energy I put forth, whatever savings I continue to accrue and reinvest, I am growing my brand. When I am out and about, whether it is with friends or amongst complete strangers, I try to keep in my consciousness that I am my brand, and people are interested in who I am. This thought process creates and provides additional opportunities for me. This process wraps around your core concepts of what you define as your level of success. Understanding the concepts of money, and having your money work for you and your best interests benefits you in the long term, and provides you with a piece of mind. Whether you are making $40,000 or $100,000 a year, this Fit helps you see common sense ways to produce additional savings.

The Physical Fit encompasses all the progress you achieved in the process of accomplishing throughout the book and its respective worksheets. Each axiom in the Physical Fit was designed to draw connections to the other three fits. I wrote the Fit in this fashion to show the connection of how each Fit and its related axioms are interchangeable and interrelated to your overall growth and development process. For everything that you seek to accomplish towards your path towards success, you must understand all your efforts are for naught if you continue to neglect your body. Your body is like a temple, a fancy sports car, and a vacation home. If you are willing to continue to put work and pour money into it to keep it operating a high level, you would be wise to do the same for ensuring that your body operates at a high level. What is the purpose of achieving all you sought to accomplish if you have stressed yourself out to the point of illness and poor health? Understanding and managing the stressors that exist in your life is critical to ensuring you can build your path towards success.

You define success by whatever means you desire. I cannot define your definition of success any much more than you could define what success is for your best friend, sibling, or a distant stranger. Another adage comes to mind, "To each their own." When I was younger, I used to think that success was a fancy car, house, and everything depicted in movies. Today, I define my success by having a carefree lifestyle, doing what I love, spending time with family and friends, and moving towards a debt-free life. Some people may affix themselves with the definition of success by having materialistic things, which is their prerogative. As long as you are comfortable with what you are doing, and you are managing yourself within the Four Fits, I believe that you will have that peace of mind that you so wish to achieve.

I have a friend of mine that I have known for well over twenty years. We worked together a long time ago. Even though we do not speak to each other as much as we used to, I always appreciated how she helped me put things in perspective. I used to be a hothead and driven by a desire to be successful. The problem was that my definition of success was also very stressful. What I had wanted did not align with my goals, dreams, and vision. I was too busy trying to achieve something that was more of a mountain with nothing to latch on to climb.

I remember vividly one conversation I had with her about where I currently was for my job and where she was with hers. I asked her if she ever thought about moving elsewhere to make more money or to have more responsibility. Her answer was very simple. She was comfortable where she was because she knew what her job entailed, had longevity at her job, and she lacked uncertainty associated with moving on elsewhere. She had her friends and support system. She had her husband and son. She is very much involved with her children's activities and the time she spends with her sister and brother. To her, she is satisfied where she is. Even though she may not have used the word, I am confident that she could describe her life as successful. She did not have to go to school for umpteenth degrees. She did not have to borrow excessively in debt. She was at peace.

During the time it took to create the concepts, axioms, and foundations for this book, I often drawback to the overall tone of the conversation I had with her. She was content on where she was. In my eyes, I looked at as very simple. Not in a demeaning way, but in a way that it made sense. Even though I still have my moments where I push and push, I recall my conversation with my friend who inadvertently provided some of the inspiration for this book. Thus, I wanted to make the book simplistic for each Fit and each axiom. For those who just want to start a foundation, I do hope that this has appealed to you and provide you some compass for your path towards success as defined by you.

I sincerely thank you for taking the time in reading this book and completing the related worksheets. In writing this book, I remember starting with a concept and watching it grow page by page as a wonderful and beautiful thing. As I continued to add an axiom and continued writing, I sought feedback from different close friends and confidants for some of the material. I thank you for your participation, as your feedback has been included in snippets throughout the book. The beauty of life is that we create and make it as whatever it is that we wish it to be. We have and always will face adversity and stress. However, the key is not to understand how to overcome adversity and stress, but how to grow yourself as a person, inside and out.

The Four Fits of Holistic Growth
Worksheets and Exercises

"The only person who can define your success is you!"

WORKSHEET #1

WHERE AM I?

EXERCISE 1: WHERE are you currently at your current stage of personal develop-ment by utilizing the Four Fits? Do you find yourself struggling in certain areas more than others? What areas do you feel like you can improve? In these four col-umns, I have provided five lines for you to describe where you are in these areas. If you want to jot down additional comments, please use the corresponding lines.

Spiritual/Mental

1. _____
2. _____
3. _____
4. _____
5. _____

Emotional

1. _____
2. _____
3. _____
4. _____
5. _____

Financial

1. _____
2. _____
3. _____
4. _____
5. _____

Physical

1. _____
2. _____
3. _____
4. _____
5. _____

Comments/Notes:

_____
_____
_____
_____
_____
_____
_____
_____

I Am My Own Most Valuable Player (M.V.P.)

EXERCISE 2: THIS is the first step under the spiritual/mental fit. Think about 12 significant accomplishments that happened in your life. Take your time to complete this exercise. Even if you have to step away for a couple of hours, or even a day to complete this because you should be able to not only jot them down, but proudly recite them out loud.

1) _____

2) _____

3) _____

4) _____

5) _____

6) _____

7) _____

8) _____

9) _____

10) _____

11) _____

Exercise 3: Write down the 12 things that you wish to accomplish in the next 12-15 months. Ensure that this list is reasonably attainable and something you can monitor throughout the year. The key is to have one item listed for each month that can be achieved no more than 4-6 weeks.

1) _____
2) _____
3) _____
4) _____
5) _____
6) _____
7) _____
8) _____
9) _____
10) _____
11) _____
12) _____

Comments/Notes:

_____
_____
_____
_____
_____
_____

THE 12 MONTHS OF PROGRESS

EXERCISE 4: You have now identified your goals to accomplish in the next 12-15 months. Rather than tuck your previous exercise away to pick it up once a month, you should make it a habit of researching what you are trying to achieve each month. The key for this exercise is to jot down three new things you have learned through your personal research. You may learn from articles, Internet, journals, documentaries, e-books, etc. to expand your knowledge of your situation. Jot down where you found that source so you can return to it whenever you may feel the need to revisit that topic again.

Goal 1_____
My Three Resources/What Did I Learn

    1) _____
    2) _____
    3) _____

Goal 2_____
My Three Resources/What Did I Learn

    1) _____
    2) _____
    3) _____

Goal 3_____
My Three Resources/What Did I Learn

    1) _____
    2) _____
    3) _____

Goal 4_____
My Three Resources/What Did I Learn

    1) _____
    2) _____
    3) _____

Goal 5_____
My Three Resources/What Did I Learn

    1) _____
    2) _____
    3) _____

Goal 6_____
My Three Resources/What Did I Learn

    1) _____
    2) _____
    3) _____

Goal 7_____
My Three Resources/What Did I Learn

    1) _____
    2) _____
    3) _____

Goal 8_____

My Three Resources/What Did I Learn

1) _____
2) _____
3) _____

Goal 9_____

My Three Resources/What Did I Learn

1) _____
2) _____
3) _____

Goal 10_____

My Three Resources/What Did I Learn

1) _____
2) _____
3) _____

Goal 11_____

My Three Resources/What Did I Learn

1) _____
2) _____
3) _____

Goal 12_____

My Three Resources/What Did I Learn

1) _____
2) _____
3) _____

THE ROAD TO BLOCKING YOUR SUCCESS IS YOU, FLUSH OUT NEGATIVITY!

EXERCISE 5: NEGATIVE energy provides obstacles to your personal development. Eliminating key areas of what negatively affects your life is easier said than done. The key is to identify what, who, how, or why such negativity exists. The purpose of this exercise is to acknowledge where does the negative energy exist, and identify a way to process that negative energy out of your life. Think of your present obstacles along your road to success, and develop creative ways to remove these obstacles to provide you growth and a sense of direction. For every negative energy, you identified, create a solution to success.

Obstacle #1
Negative Energy_____
Solution to Success_____

Obstacle #2
Negative Energy_____
Solution to Success_____

Obstacle #3
Negative Energy_____
Solution to Success_____

Obstacle #4
Negative Energy_____
Solution to Success_____

Obstacle #5
Negative Energy_____
Solution to Success_____

Obstacle #6
Negative Energy_____
Solution to Success_____

WORKSHEET #5

TURNING A DREAM INTO A VISION AND A VISION INTO REALITY

EXERCISE 6: THERE is nothing wrong with dreaming. The world is full of dreamers. We need more people of vision. Are you a visionary? What are your three and five-year plans? In this exercise, you should think of at least five goals you intend to accomplish in your first three years, and then build upon that in constructing your five-year vision. Note how the word "construct" is used and not "wish." Becoming active and forward-thinking visionaries will mean that you take some risks and creating something steady to build upon from your projected 12-month goals.

My Three-Year Vision:

1) _____
2) _____
3) _____
4) _____
5) _____

My Five-Year Vision:

1) _____
2) _____
3) _____
4) _____
5) _____

Exercise 7: After writing down your visions for your next three and five years, write down what you believe would assist you in achieving your vision. Think of some resources that may assist you in this journey. Think as to what is in your community, library, the Internet, volunteer opportunities, and free courses provided in your community that may provide you with an opportunity for newfound knowledge.

1) _____
2) _____
3) _____
4) _____
5) _____
6) _____
7) _____
8) _____
9) _____
10) _____

Remember, you are more than welcome to revise your visions as necessary. However, you should provide something that will provide you a feeling of significant accomplishment, reward yourself for determination, and a source of personal pride.

WORKSHEET #6

THE TRUTH SHOULD NOT HURT

EXERCISE 8: YOUR perceptions of past failings pave the way for future opportunities. We do not often get what we want in life. That is reality. However, the opportunities we felt at that time that was best for us did not materialize. Despite this fact, this may have paved the way for opportunities you may not have been aware of at that moment. In this exercise, identify five situations where you may have felt that an opportunity or event may have slipped away that has meaning to you, and what did you learn from that experience.

1) _____

_____

2) _____

_____

3) _____

_____

4) _____

_____

5) _____

_____

THE DIFFERENCES BETWEEN WANTS AND WOULD LIKE IS WITHIN YOUR MIND

EXERCISE 9: IN determining what you would like and what you want, you will see that there are distinct differences. The differences should involve something you wish to achieve but are willing to make adjustments or take an alternative version of what you seek to achieve. In this exercise, list your wants in one column and then what you would like in another column. Do not limit yourself to one specific area, think about what you desire and what you want to achieve. From there, begin populating the lists.

What I Want Is…..

1) _____
2) _____
3) _____
4) _____
5) _____

What I Would Like Is…..

1) _____
2) _____
3) _____
4) _____
5) _____

REMOVING YOUR EMOTIONS WHEN MAKING DECISIONS STARTS WITHIN YOU

EXERCISE #9: THIS exercise focuses on the process of removing your emotions from your decision making. The challenge we have as humans is that our emotions may sometimes cloud our judgment. Although there is nothing wrong being emotional by nature, learning how to keep a steady head, steady mind, and steady heart creates additional opportunities for growth from within. Think of situations or scenarios where you may have had made a hasty decision based on emotions and provide a self-evaluation of what you could do in the future.

Situation A:_____

What could I have done differently?_____

_____

The next time I have a similar situation I can/should do_____

_____

_____

Situation B:_____

What could I have done differently?_____

_____

The next time I have a similar situation I can/should do_____

_____

_____

Situation C:_____

What could I have done differently?_____

_____

The next time I have a similar situation I can/should do_____

_____

_____

Situation D:_____

What could I have done differently?_____

_____

The next time I have a similar situation I can/should do_____

_____

_____

Relax, Unwind, and Take Time for You

Exercise #10: If you do not take the time to take care of yourself or tend to your mental needs, you will burn out. It is important that you take time for yourself. Unplug yourself from your busy schedule, activities, and immerse yourself in something that provides you a release from the world. The key to this exercise is to discover activities for yourself that are independent of another person or entity in which you truly find yourself in a state of peace and serenity. The key to this exercise is to identify what these activities are and act on them in an independent fashion.

Stressors in my Life:

1) _____
2) _____
3) _____
4) _____
5) _____

Activities/Hobbies:

1) _____
2) _____
3) _____
4) _____
5) _____

YOUR LOVE RESUME

EXERCISE #11: IN this light-hearted exercise, you are seeking for a different type of job. This job involves looking at you in a relationship aspect and applying for another's heart and mind. I have provided a sample resume template to fill out. Use some creativity in completing this exercise.

Summary of Accomplishments

_____

_____

_____

Skills/Notable Abilities

_____

_____

_____

Notable Accomplishments

_____

_____

_____

Why Should I Be Offered This Position?

_____

_____

_____

What Does My Partner Seek That I Should Continue to Improve?

_____

_____

_____

THE FINANCIAL CESSPOOL –
CREDIT CARDS AND SHORT TERM LOANS

EXERCISE 12: IN this exercise, you will do some research. You will need to pull each credit card statement, car loan, and determine how much you are paying towards the debt, and how much interest you are paying each month. After you finish jotting down the numbers, calculate how much interest you are paying each month, and the percentage of your minimum payments are toward interest.

Card/Debt 1:_____

Minimum Payment_____**Interest Paid Per Month**_____**APR**_____

Card/Debt 1:_____

Minimum Payment_____**Interest Paid Per Month**_____**APR**_____

Card/Debt 1:_____

Minimum Payment_____**Interest Paid Per Month**_____**APR**_____

Card/Debt 1:_____

Minimum Payment_____**Interest Paid Per Month**_____**APR**_____

Card/Debt 1:_____

Minimum Payment_____**Interest Paid Per Month**_____**APR**_____

Card/Debt 1:_____

Minimum Payment_____**Interest Paid Per Month**_____**APR**_____

Card/Debt 1:_____

Minimum Payment_____Interest Paid Per Month_____APR_____

Card/Debt 1:_____

Minimum Payment_____Interest Paid Per Month_____APR_____

Total Minimum Payments_____

Total Interest Paid_____

Percentage of Interest Paid* _____

*To calculate the percentage, take the total interest paid and divide it by total minimum payments owed. Therefore, if you paid a total of $423 out of $742 in minimum payments, you would have 57% of your payments that go towards interest.

WORKSHEET #12

MY LIFE'S VICES

EXERCISE 13: *IN this exercise, you will focus on some of the vices that affect your spending and consumption. By identifying what you are "vices" are, you will be able to identify and target areas where you can create savings. This exercise is broken into three different phases and will require you to look at your last 3-6 months to complete this exercise. Three months will give you a small snapshot. Six months will provide a more realist outlook into building your brand.*

My tool for tracking my spending:_____

My Top Five Vices (Top Five Spending Categories) and Amounts:

1) _____
2) _____
3) _____
4) _____
5) _____

25% Rule – Take each of the categories above and write down the 25% savings…

1) _____
2) _____
3) _____
4) _____
5) _____
   Total Savings_____

Now identify three ways you can pass those savings into growing your own brand...

1) _____

2) _____

3) _____

WORKSHEET #13

STRESS MANAGEMENT COMES FROM STRESS IDENTIFICATION

EXERCISE 14: RECOGNIZING the stressors in your life and learning how to address them helps improve your mental and physical health. Exposure to stressful events and situations are inevitable. Therefore, you must develop coping methods and ways to decompress the stress from within. In this first exercise of this worksheet, you are to identify three stressors in your general life, relationships with others, and in the workplace. Please note that in determining the stressors in your place of work, this may extend to your relationship with others instead of a dating or marital relationship.

General Stressors:

1) _____
2) _____
3) _____

Interpersonal Relationship Stressors:

1) _____
2) _____
3) _____

Workplace Stressors:

1) _____
2) _____
3) _____

Exercise 15: Stress in the workplace is more common than any other stress. This is due to the majority of your days, weeks, and months involve some process relating to work whether it is coming and going to work; your relationship with your supervisor and coworkers, customer service, target goals, and overall performance. In this exercise, you will look at your workplace stressors you indicated above, and develop a strategy to transition from your stressors at work to build the bridge between work and life.

1) _____
2) _____
3) _____

Exercise 16: How well do you manage stress throughout the week. This activity expands from the one above by having you come up with several coping strategies when confronted with a stressful event. If you have something that has been stressing you out throughout the day or week, develop a way to recognize that stressor and ways to cope.

1) _____
2) _____
3) _____
4) _____
5) _____

MY LIFE MATTERS

EXERCISE 15: YOU only live once. It is up to you to make the most of that opportunity. Even though we should all live for the moment, we must take care of ourselves. At some point in time, we will have minor ailments or illnesses. If we do not take care of them immediately or within a reasonable amount of time, the acute illnesses become chronic. Your willingness to work with your physician and managing your illnesses will bode well for your overall wealth. In this exercise, identify your chronic ailments, and any health issues that you may have had over the past year and what have you done to address them. Identify as to whether or not you are taking medication or continuing to follow up appointments. Also, identify your dentist appointments and any recommendations from a healthcare professional.

My primary physician:_____

Last Appointment:_____

My dentist:_____

Last Appointment:_____

Specialist info:_____

Chronic Ailments and recommended treatment/medication:

 1) _____

 2) _____

 3) _____

Strategies to combat/alleviate your chronic ailments:

1) _____

2) _____

3) _____

Made in the USA
Middletown, DE
09 May 2022